DON'T SLEEP ON IT

Praise for *Don't Sleep on It*

"Kavit doesn't just talk the talk. He walks the walk. His lessons have been distilled here in a crisp and easy read!"

—**Shama Hyder**, best-selling author of
The Zen of Social Media Marketing & Momentum

"This book contains solid ideas that I know work and will work for many years to come. If you're an experienced entrepreneur, this book will remind you of a dozen things you know you should be doing and rapidly focus you on taking action. If you're starting out, this book might seem simple but let me assure you, it takes real experience and expertise to make something simple and that's what you've got here. Best of all, I like the respect and consideration for the customer that shines through in this book. Kavit sees marketing as an act of service. He never loses sight of the fact that we're dealing with real people who consume our content, explore our websites and trust us with their purchasing decisions. Other than being the right approach, It's the only approach that works."

—**Daniel Priestley**, best-selling author of
Entrepreneur Revolution, Oversubscribed and 24Assets

"Kavit Haria's principles are powerful. They work. This will transform your business."

—**Mark Anastasi,** author of the *New York Times*
Bestseller *The Laptop Millionaire*

"Kavit is a rare breed—a super smart businessman with real heart and soul. He has a proven methodology for taking businesses online and a willingness to genuinely help others that I have seen and experienced for myself. There is an awful lot of 'noise' out in the online business environment right now. If you are serious about turning your passions into profits, look no further than this book for a clear, honest and systematic approach!"

—**Kelly Teasdale**, Founder, Market My Product Ltd

"There has never been a better time in history to start a business. Kavit shows you the steps to do it right, make a profit, and avoid painful pitfalls."

—**Tom Schwab**, CEO Interview Valet

"What I love about Kavit is his authentic desire to truly help people with their own success in the shortest time possible. His book is an absolute perfect resource for building, growing and scaling a business built around your expertise the right way. If you are a coach, consultant or expert, you need this book!"

—**Casey Zeman**, Best Selling Author of *Build Your Audience with Live Video*

"I have had the pleasure of knowing Kavit for some time now and what struck me when I first met him was his unconditional desire to make a difference. He comes from a genuine place of wanting to impact people for good and his creative, high level thinking has enabled thousands to have been positively impacted, and to positively impact, as a result. He was one of the first people to introduce me to the concept that entrepreneurs have the ability have the biggest impact on humanity as a result of the actions we take with utilising the knowledge we already hold. This is something which has had a profound impact on myself and how I operate. Kavit is a humble, talented, big thinker that has the ability to not only impact you but thousands around the world."

—**Will Polston**, Founder *The Elite Network*

"Kavit's knowledge of business, product creation and marketing is shared is second to none. I introduced him to Infusionsoft six years ago and he quickly applied his marketing and online expertise to this powerful platform, culminating in his Automated Business System concept. This book contains many valuable gems that you should read and, most importantly, take action on."

—**Adrian Savage**, The Automation Architect

"Kavit is right on the money with this book. If you follow his instructions, you will find a proven process to turn your passion and expertise into a profitable, scalable and enjoyable online business. This is a must read!"

—**Daven Michaels**, author of the *New York Times*
and Amazon best-seller, *Outsource Smart: Be Your Own
Boss Without Letting Your Business Become The Boss Of You*

"Kavit has a calm, grounded, centred, open energy which affects the state and energy of others very positively. His practical strategies are introduced to others with a real honesty as to whether they fit the client's needs… these are rare values."

—**Nicki Vee**, Master Coach Trainer

"This book is excellent! In it, Kavit breaks down exactly what you need to do to create a thriving expert business in a clear, step-by-step format. His break down of how to uncover your true value to a client (which is something most everyone in the expert space struggles with) is the best I've ever seen. I even shared that and a couple of other insights from that with my seven and eight figure clients and they were blown away by the material just like I was (I hope you don't mind Kavit!). Bottom line: get this book and your income and impact promises to soar!"

—**Ron Reich**, The World's #1 Product Launch Specialist

"This is a simple and direct way to further your growth as a business, if you want to gain further positioning as an expert in your field this is the book to read! Kavit truly cares and you can really feel that come through in the book. A must read for all."

—**Elliot Kay**, Author, *Power To Succeed*

"If you want to create an income by sharing your expertise in a way that reaches many people at once, this book will show you how. Kavit's clear thinking provides a distraction-free framework for you to leverage what you know and build a profitable business."

—**John Lee Dumas**, host of the *Entrepreneur on Fire* podcast

"I've watched Kavit grow as a person and as an entrepreneur for a decade online. And while much has changed on the internet and marketing products and services online, one thing has remained constant, Kavit's care for his customers and helping them to achieve the business and life they desire. That will always win and why you must read every word in his new book so you can succeed in the next 10+ years of your own life."

—**Greg Rollett**, Emmy Award Winning Producer and Founder of *Ambitious*

"I've seen Kavit work with people and turn their ideas and expertise into businesses for over 8 years now. He is very informed, at the cutting edge and knows how to make a business profitable. If you want to earn from your passion and expertise and contribute to the world, you need to read this book!"

—**Sohial Khan**, author of *Guerrilla Marketing and Joint Ventures*

"Having followed Kavit over the last several years, what I most admire is his resilience and the clarity with which he sees things which have helped him strategically see the best ways to market various business opportunities. There are many one-hit wonders in the marketing world, however, over the past decade Kavit has proved time and time again, he is not one of them."

—**Beejel Parmar**, Rapid Progress Mentor

"With this book, Kavit shows you exactly how to profit from your expertise online. Kavit really understands that so much of what makes a great business is about attitude—towards your customers, your product creation and your marketing. This is a must read if you're thinking of launching your services online."

—**Nick James**, Founder of Seriously Fun Business Ltd

"Every time I experience Kavit sharing his knowledge around creating value for others and productizing it I learn something new. I'm always eager to find out what I'm going to learn next!"

—**Phil MacNevin**, CEO Lift Media

"Kavit is the consummate professional and really knows his stuff about creating well-crafted expert courses and how to sell them to attract high paying clients. I have personally benefited from Kavit's consulting and I know you will too, so I can highly recommend this book."

—**Arvind Devalia**, best-selling author of *Get The Life You Love*

"I absolutely love the clarity of Kavit's thinking and process. He is able to explain how to start an online business from scratch and make it profitable, scalable and predictable in a very simple way."

—**Simone Vincenzi**, host of the *Explode Your Coaching Biz* podcast

"Kavit has the pulse of the industry and I highly recommend you devour every word in this book."

—**Clinton Swaine**, CEO Frontier Training

"I have spoken on various occasions at different events with Kavit, and each time he is presenting on stage I sit quietly at the back of the room making notes! Kavit has a rare skill to simply the complex, break down the complicated, and navigate creating a successful online business into easy to manage bite-size chunks!"

—**Chris Farrell**, respected internet marketing mentor

DON'T SLEEP ON IT

Turn Your Passion & Expertise into a Profitable Online Business

KAVIT HARIA

NEW YORK

LONDON • NASHVILLE • MELBOURNE • VANCOUVER

DON'T SLEEP ON IT
Turn Your Passion & Expertise into
a Profitable Online Business

© 2018 **KAVIT HARIA**

Published in New York, New York, by Morgan James Publishing. Morgan James is a trademark of Morgan James, LLC. www.MorganJamesPublishing.com

The Morgan James Speakers Group can bring authors to your live event. For more information or to book an event visit The Morgan James Speakers Group at www.TheMorganJamesSpeakersGroup.com.

ISBN 978-1-68350-985-1 paperback
ISBN 978-1-68350-986-8 eBook
Library of Congress Control Number: 2018934577

Cover Design by:
Rachel Lopez
www.r2cdesign.com

Interior Design by:
Bonnie Bushman
The Whole Caboodle Graphic Design

In an effort to support local communities, raise awareness and funds, Morgan James Publishing donates a percentage of all book sales for the life of each book to Habitat for Humanity Peninsula and Greater Williamsburg.

Get involved today! Visit
www.MorganJamesBuilds.com

Dedication

Dedicated to Bhaishree:
your impeccable clarity of vision keeps me focused on the truth.

Table of Contents

Acknowledgements

This book has been in the works for two years. Whilst the planning and writing is done alone, it's typically the result of many collaborative efforts. I am deeply grateful for each person who contributed in lending their wisdom to this book.

I would like to thank my *Automated Business System* clients. You trust us to help you launch and build your business online and together we shall continue to inspire millions of people around the world. Special thanks to the clients I've shared stories about in the book; you helped bring the book to life.

Also a big thanks to my *Automated Business System* team; every one of you plays a crucial role in creating meaningful work that changes the world. Thank you for the openness, honesty and creativity you bring to every encounter. You are all changing the online landscape as we know it and you continue to stretch and inspire me every day.

I am grateful for my editor, Kim Farnell, who took my ideas and helped me carve out a strong manuscript, staying on point and on deadline. You helped raise the quality of the book. Thanks to Luke Kelly, my trusted designer for many years. You helped bring the book to life with the amazing cover. Thanks also to David Hancock, Margo Toulouse and the rest of the team at Morgan James Publishing for helping me turn what originally started out as a Google Doc file into a beautiful book, available to experts and changemakers all around the world.

A special thank you to Suhani, Menka and Ajay. You have all been so encouraging with your intriguing questions and your enthusiastic, open and honest feedback. You helped shape the book in more ways than you know and I will always be grateful.

Introduction

I have a definition of success. For me, it's very simple. It's not about wealth and fame and power. It's about how many shining eyes I have around me.

—**Benjamin Zander**, *The Art of Possibility*

Benjamin Zander is a conductor for the Boston Philharmonic Orchestra. In his book *The Art of Possibility* he describes the experience of bringing together a group of talented musicians to create a beautiful work of art. He knows he's doing his job when the musicians are performing to the best of their ability and feeling the excitement of doing their best work.

Of course, you don't have to conduct an orchestra to make others come alive. If you've ever played even a small part in helping someone overcome a barrier to their health, business or financial problems, or spiritual issues—or anything else that contributes towards their happiness—you'll know the joy of seeing the twinkle return to their eyes.

The World Needs More of this

When you light a fire in someone else, you can change the world. We don't have to wait for politicians; we can change things by helping people overcome problems, and this positive impact affects their wider communities.

This may sound hopelessly idealistic, but think about it for a second. A doctor may realise that instead of prescribing medication for health conditions caused by being overweight, she could help a person understand their body, manage their mindset and eat more healthily. By doing so, she gives that person the gift of a stronger and healthier body for the rest of their life. With more energy and better health they'll be less reliant on others for help, able to do more for their family and friends, and they might teach others to eat more healthily themselves.

In other words, for each person who benefits from this doctor's advice, maybe ten or more experience a small or even significant improvement in their quality of life.

If you've ever helped someone overcome a problem, you've probably had a small insight into the effect it has on their family and friends. And you'll know how addictive this experience can be. Once you've helped a few people, you'll be driven to help even more.

Don't Sleep On It!, is a call for you to unleash what you know. You have something to offer. You have something that's incredibly valuable to someone else. Whether you know it or not, what you know at this time is what someone else needs in order to overcome their challenges, remedy their pain, or solve their problem.

My spiritual and meditation teacher, Bhaishree, often reminds me that my days are finite. We will never know when life takes us away, and there is no better time than today to do the work that matters. One day, your life will be no more.

We tend to live life *without* the urgency that this basic fact of life provides. 'There will always be tomorrow,' we say. It is a stubborn illusion. But right now, somewhere around the world, maybe even right under your nose, there are people who will benefit from what you know. This is not the time to sleep on it.

If you feel you have something to give, or a nagging sense that you have more to contribute, whether it's something you've been doing already or something you're ready to step into, there really has been no better time to start putting it into motion.

Don't Sleep On It! could easily be misunderstood to mean that you have to make decisions in haste and leave the security of your day job to pursue an entrepreneurial path filled with incredible reward and risk. But that is not what I mean.

Don't Sleep On It! isn't about getting everything done today. It is not about overworking or overwhelming yourself and forgetting about every other part of life. Working like a maniac is often counterproductive, too. It is about making a conscious decision to look objectively at what you know, and what you need to learn, and realise that there is a large group of people that you can serve with your expertise.

You have a responsibility to turn your passions and expertise into a force for good, and no one else, but yourself, can make this contribution. Sitting on the sidelines and not leading with who you are and what you know will rob the world of the contribution you can make. The cost of inaction is unfathomable. As Todd Henry says in his book, *The Accidental Creative*, 'Don't die full of your best work.'

There will be times when you begin to rethink your value, package your knowledge and create your business where taking time away will actually enhance the work that you do. In fact, at times, sleeping on it will be the only option available to you. It might seem counterintuitive that the best way to get your mind working is to sleep, but a good night's sleep can provide the space for your unconscious mind to process the work you completed during the day, helping you to see if anything is missing, and preparing you for efficiently continuing on your quest to share.

Providing Solutions

In this book, you're going to learn how to create and effectively market and sell your expertise with an automated business that reaches more people, saves you time and makes you money while you sleep.

I'm going to teach you the basics of a successful expert business: how to identify your most valuable knowledge and determine who it's most valuable *to*. Then we're going to look at how to leverage your expertise by creating an online course and your own personal expert brand. You'll learn, step-by-step, how to create an automated sales funnel that helps clients get to know you and trust you until they're ready to buy, and discover the marketing solutions I use to draw traffic to my website.

The philosophies I use in my flagship service, the *Automated Business System,* help my clients establish successful and sustainable online businesses based on their expertise. In this programme, my clients use their professional expertise to create an automated business to help people overcome a problem or achieve an important goal. Using automation and the power of the internet to reach people all over the world, they no longer experience any limits on their income or—more importantly—the number of people they're able to +help.

You are an Expert

Every one of us has at least one area of expertise—some important insight, knowledge, talent or skill—that can change people's lives in a significant way.

The doctor I described earlier is a client of mine. Dr Julie Coffey is a family doctor who studied natural health material when she developed early-onset arthritis, a painful condition that conventional medicine couldn't easily treat. As she made changes to her lifestyle and diet, her joints improved and she also had more energy and lost weight effortlessly. She soon realised what she'd learned was valuable to others and started to suggest alternative health solutions to her patients. Only a few tried her suggestions. Working with us, she realised she didn't have to restrict herself to this tiny group but could extend her new knowledge to thousands of people by creating an online course.

Expertise doesn't always come with a certificate. It can, of course, but although Dr Coffey is an 'expert' as a medical doctor, it was her personal research and her new diet and lifestyle that gave her something special to share with the world.

You don't just become an expert simply because you have a piece of paper saying so. In fact, many experts don't have that piece of paper at all! Like Dr Coffey, you may have had a problem to solve, or perhaps you had such a burning desire to learn something you spent thousands of pounds and years of your time in developing your new skill.

For example, Micah Lipsmeyer, another of my clients, tried playing the guitar and was hooked. He loved it so much that he pushed through the awkwardness and embarrassment of starting out, and kept learning and practising despite fifteen-hour shifts on a construction site. Years later, he worked out how to break down the skills to teach other people who were aching to play.

Through his struggle to learn, and his efforts to simplify the process for other people, Micah became an expert in playing the guitar, and thanks to her determination to find a better solution to her joint pain than a replacement knee, Dr Coffey became an expert in weight loss and healthy eating. In other cases, a person becomes an expert simply by doing their job, day in and day out.

Take Sam Oke. He's a recruitment consultant with over a decade of experience as a traditional recruiter, helping people with their CVs and getting them into jobs. He observed a wave of finding and hiring great talent thanks to LinkedIn, and realised that people need to have stronger LinkedIn profiles, more than just CVs. So he set out to write and put together winning LinkedIn profiles for his clients and they began to get hired. Now he offers a simple LinkedIn profile rewriting service at linkedcareergrowth.com. His business focuses on North Americans and his clients of this service are getting found and interviewed and hired quickly at top firms thanks to an effective LinkedIn profile.

Expertise doesn't come easily. To become an expert takes effort and time, yet many people continue to undervalue their expertise because their knowledge is so natural to them it's hard to remember how things were when they were starting out. They overlook the years of effort and energy invested in learning and practising, and forget that other people don't know what they know.

This doesn't serve anyone. Once you've overcome the hurdles to understand how something works, you're able to give others the fast-track route to your knowledge without the painful trial and error you had to go through. Imagine how much easier Micah's life might have been if he had been able to reach his goal in just ninety days! How much money and time could he have saved? It sounds farfetched but this is now what he teaches in his online course, *90 Day Guitar* (90DayGuitar.com).

Make Sharing Your Expertise Your Priority

Your knowledge is valuable because it allows others to overcome the same problems you once faced, faster and more easily than you managed yourself. If you could break down what you learned and share it with other people, you'd play your part in changing the world.

Todd Henry says in his book *Die Empty*, 'Your worth as a person transcends the value you create, but your work is the most visible expression of your priorities.' Do you intend to carry on as you are, or share your learning with as many people as you can?

Many people will have a go. They'll advise friends and family or create a small business serving as many clients as their schedule allows. But if you know something that helps other people to overcome a difficulty or achieve an important lifetime ambition, it becomes part of your purpose to share it with as many people as you can. You cannot sleep on it. Like Jeff Walker, author of *Launch: An Internet Millionaire's Secret Formula to Sell Almost Anything Online, Build a Business You Love and Live the Life of Your Dreams*, says, 'The world has changed, and the only true security is your ability to create value and get paid for that value.

This Won't be Easy

Setting up and launching a leveraged business doesn't have to be hard; you simply need the right elements in place and working as they should. To get the best from this book, don't just read the chapters, but make the time to implement the action steps, particularly at the information gathering stage. This isn't the sexy part of the process, but it will help you avoid investing weeks or months of effort into a course nobody buys.

I'll be honest with you; this isn't something you'll achieve in a weekend. It will take hard work and determination to build your product, automate your sales process and persist with the marketing long after the pieces are in place. If money is the only thing that drives you, it's unlikely to sustain your energy and focus for as long as it takes.

I love this quote from Mark Nepo's *The Book of Awakening*. It reminds me to make a difference, but in a small way—not to exceed my boundaries, but to immerse myself in work that lights me up so I can bring this energy to the people I serve.

All I can ask of this work is that it comes over you the way the ocean covers a stone stuck in the open, that it surprises and refreshes, that it makes you or me glisten, and leaves us scoured as we are, just softer for the moment and more clear.

When you're working, try to recall the passion and determination that drove you to develop the knowledge or skill you're about to share. Imagine it's your role to awaken the same drive in others and to see them succeed and take their learning further than you are able to reach. If your expertise has changed your life, you can be sure it will help others, too.

Let's get on with it!

Kavit Haria

PART ONE

BUSINESS FUNDAMENTALS

There are two valuable strategies that underpin everything I do. Each one requires a fundamental mindset shift you can take forward into the processes of branding your business and creating, selling and marketing your course.

First, you need to think differently about what you think your time is worth. If you don't break free from the money-for-time mindset, you'll never feel comfortable earning considerably more money, despite investing fewer hours of your time. A shift in mindset also helps you focus on creating the highest possible value for your client without spending more time.

Secondly, you should look at your clients in detail, creating a 'customer avatar', which will act as a key source of information when you write your courses and content. The better you understand your client, the easier it will be to write, market and sell courses that get real results. One of the biggest challenges an expert faces is moving away from what they *think* people should know, to what their clients *actually want to achieve.* Once you're able to make this shift, your fortune will change dramatically.

As you read on, consider your own situation, experience and expertise. In particular, think about how these might relate to creating a product that has amazing value in your clients' eyes, something they're willing to pay for without consulting you personally.

The people who can make the greatest changes in the world are experts, changemakers and entrepreneurs. Every changemaker has within them a seed of potential that (if unleashed) will help people change a specific area of their life.

When an expert leverages their knowledge and skills by offering products and services online, they have the potential to not only change their own life, but the lives of hundreds of clients, and potentially their clients' friends and family, too. My hope is that by working with a changemaker like you to realise this goal, I play my own part in transforming society, compounding to millions of people globally.

Chapter One

Rethinking Your Value

Don't tell people how good you make the goods; tell them how good your goods make them.

—Leo Burnett

Think about the value of your product or service to your client. It might seem obvious to you, but it's important you know exactly why they find your product valuable. That way, you'll be able to communicate the reasons they should buy it instead of another that looks similar.

Great marketers know that people don't buy products. (Before you start pointing out the Black Friday crush in technology stores with people fighting each other for a big screen TV, let me explain.) Of course, people purchase products, but there's a reason for each purchase that has little to do with the products themselves.

When someone pays for a product or service, they are buying two things:

- The *result* they expect
- *Why* you're helping them achieve the result

To put this into context properly, we need to understand how human behaviour is influenced. Simon Sinek, the author of *Start With Why*, explains that people are influenced by either inspiration or manipulation. We see manipulation everywhere—discounted sales, scarcity sales ploys, advertising that urges you to buy now, etc. And there's a reason for this; manipulation works!

Yet it doesn't always bring long-term success, client loyalty and long term happiness. The aim, instead, should be to inspire loyal customers. Kevin Kelly, co-founding editor of *Wired* magazine, in his seminal essay '1,000 True Fans', discusses how you can turn your passion or expertise into income by serving a small, loyal audience. In short, you don't need a million followers; you only need a thousand 'true fans' who love what you do. And that comes from *inspiration*, not *manipulation*.

Simon Sinek introduced the concept of the Golden Circle to explain how we can inspire rather than manipulate, and this is most important at the start of your journey when you're rethinking your value.

The Golden Circle demonstrates that every company in the world knows WHAT they do (they can easily describe their product or service). Some companies know HOW they do what they do (they know how they stand out). Yet few companies can share WHY they do what they do ('making money' isn't enough).

Most new business owners are drawn to design the features of their product as the first thing they do. Careful product design is essential (we'll discuss course creation in Chapter Four), but deep down your potential clients don't really care about features. They want to know what working with you will enable them to achieve and what makes *you* the right person to work with.

If you can explain **why** you're offering what you offer and the result it produces, you're onto a winner. That's what people buy. That's what people want.

Trading **Hours** for **Outcomes**

You are responsible for serving your clients in the best way you can. You need to create a situation where you have the financial resources, energy and time to create life-changing products, listen to your clients' concerns and give them the answers they need. This means taking care of yourself so you have it within yourself to take care of your clients.

Most people with a job are paid for turning up, nine to five, Monday to Friday. When you're paid for your time, it doesn't matter how much work you get done, only that you spend the agreed number of hours sitting at your desk.

Obviously, if you got nothing done you'd probably be disciplined and eventually lose your job—but in the meantime you'd still get paid. The system is designed to pay you for the amount of time you're present at work. Many people establish an online business because they want to break free from being stuck in an office day in and day out, but some of the practices they bring with them, such as being paid by the hour, set them up for long hours and limited rewards.

Many coaches, consultants, or people teaching a particular skill or expertise still continue to charge in this way because it seems like the most obvious or fairest thing to do. Anyone moving from a low hourly wage working for a large company to charging a higher hourly rate for their services as a self-employed professional is likely to feel pleased with the increase in pay.

However, it's soon obvious that in working for yourself you must spend a lot more time managing the day-to-day hustle of bringing in work, and this reduces the number of hours for which you're actually paid. To earn more money, you may have to make a significant hike on your hourly rate.

This brings us to the real difficulty with charging per hour: in many industries, there's a limit to how much people are willing to pay. Online, where clients have access to service providers from all over the world, the market can drive your rate down even lower. You end up working more hours to keep your business ticking over and have little energy for the product or service you're working to sell.

Leveraging your expertise involves setting yourself up differently in your clients' minds—redefining your value so they buy outcomes, not hours. This not only allows you to charge more for your services but motivates your clients to push through the difficult times because they have a vision of success in their minds.

Tim Harper was already over forty when he hit the ski slopes for the first time. When he first managed to navigate a basic blue run without injuring himself or others, he had no idea he'd be a qualified ski instructor a few years down the line. But he became so captivated by the experience that he knuckled down to the gruelling practice necessary to succeed in the sport.

Now, selling his exclusive membership group and skiing skills video course online, Tim recalls the first time he saw a talented skier making light work of a challenging run:

'He was creating perfect tracks and making the whole thing look easy, almost as though he had been born with skis on his feet; a far cry from the ugly technique I had developed by teaching myself. Watching this incredible skiing God in total awe, I became determined to become just as good, so skiing would become as natural as walking to me.'

The ease and grace with which this experienced skier navigated the slopes was the inspiration that set Tim on the path to becoming the accomplished skier and successful instructor he is today. He could imagine himself gliding effortlessly down the difficult runs, enjoying the sound of his skis on the snow and the beautiful white spray that followed his every turn. This carried him forward through the difficult times.

When Tim invested in skiing lessons, ski passes and expensive hotels and flights, he wasn't buying these things. He was spending his money on achieving his dream.

Rule number one of a leveraged business is that it doesn't let the market dictate its value based on an hour of the business owner's time. Instead, it creates a product that doesn't need the expert to be present—which would limit availability and drive up the price—but still leads to an outcome the client is desperate to achieve.

We've all seen this concept at work—from cars that promise adventure to perfumes that suggest glamour and romance—and it's often associated with unscrupulous sales techniques. But if your business genuinely helps people succeed in overcoming a problem or achieving a goal, rethinking your value helps more people benefit from your expertise.

Visualise Your Clients' Outcomes

When my clients start working on the *Automated Business System*, they start with a strategic exercise I call 'Mapping Realities', which helps them direct their products towards an outcome that increases the value in their clients' minds.

This exercise assumes that your product or service will create a transformation and produce a desired result for your client. *The client's reality after this transformation will be different from the reality they are currently in.* Your client's **current reality** (on the left of the diagram below) contains some form of pain or dissatisfaction, whereas their **ideal reality** (on the right) occurs when they have consumed your product or service and the pain has removed.

In building your product, you must think deeply and empathetically about your client's experiences, emotions, feelings and thought patterns *before* consuming your product (when life is difficult) and *after* (when things are better or easier.)

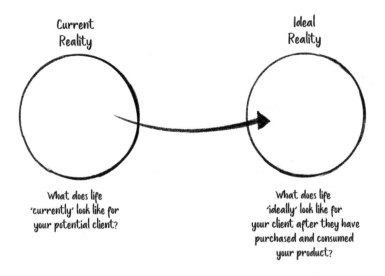

Once you start getting results for your clients, it's easier to paint a picture of the outcome your product or service achieves, but it takes empathy and insight to understand their problem when the thing they want comes easily to you. The more you can put yourself in their shoes and understand the transformation your product provides, the easier it is to:

- Understand what truly matters to your client and how important the transformation is to them
- Realise how small or big the gap is from their current reality to where they want to be

- Uncover the exact areas of learning your clients requires (this will help you map out your content as well as fuel your social media strategies)
- Discover the language they use so you can take these ideas and use them in your marketing and sales collateral—thereby increasing your conversions

Often, a person's ideal reality is based on another person's success, which shows up a problem in their own lives. For example, Tim Harper was already having a great skiing holiday, but when he saw a professional skier in action, he realised how poor his self-taught technique was in comparison and he knew exactly how good he'd like to be. When Dr Julie Coffey changed her diet and her lifestyle, many people noticed how she had lost weight and had more energy and zest for life, and they wanted to know how to achieve this themselves.

By completing the Mapping Realities exercise, Tim, Julie and all our other clients can visualise their client's journey, step by step, based on their own path to success.

This single exercise has the power to transform your entire business. Once you understand the two realities, you can create and offer a product or service that bridges a gap from one to the other, guaranteeing client satisfaction and increasing your sales opportunities.

Differentiation—Why are *You* Special?

As I showed earlier, people buy products for two reasons: the results they expect and who provides that result.

The Mapping Realities exercise ensures you're not only clear on the outcomes but also that there are no missing steps in your process that might cause your client to fail. This gives you a reliable product that delivers an ideal result, but it may still not be enough to convince your clients to buy.

With the rapid growth and sheer scale of the internet, if you've found a solution to an urgent problem—unless you're extremely lucky—you won't be alone. And if you are, you won't be for long.

Joseph Michael is an expert who had the whole internet to himself for a short while. He created 'Learn Scrivener Fast', a course teaching writers to use one of the most powerful, but most mind-boggling pieces of writing software on the market. Despite its popularity, Michael discovered there was almost no support information and the learning curve was steep and painful. When he launched his course in a niche market, it was huge, because there wasn't a single other course promising to make Scrivener easy for new users.

Now, more than three years later, a number of 'me too' products are creeping on the market and they brazenly claim to be the most authoritative, the most comprehensive or the best way to learn Scrivener. This happens in every industry, demonstrating there is always room for more.

It's important to get over the idea that your product must be different, because no matter how much of a revelation your learning has been to you, others will have realised the same thing and will promise results similar to yours. As the internet makes it easy for clients to shop around, something else must set you apart.

That something is you.

Dan Sullivan, founder of Strategic Coach, calls this Unique Ability, and defines it in this way: 'First, it is a superior ability that other people notice and value; second, we love doing it and want to do it as much as possible; third, it is energising both for us and others around us; and, fourth, we keep getting better, never running out of possibilities for further improvement.'

In his blog,[1] Cameron Herold, author of *Double Double: How To Double Your Revenue In 3 Years Or Less* provides an exercise to help you work out your unique ability by working through the following steps:

- Make a list of everything you do daily and weekly.
- List these items in the first column of a spreadsheet.
- In the second column, add one of these four letters describing your skill level related to the task:
  - I = incompetent (you're terrible at it)
  - C = competent (you're OK at it)
  - E = excellent (you're awesome at it—but you don't love it)
  - U = unique ability (as described by Dan Sullivan above)
- In the third column, put the hourly wage you'd be willing to pay someone to do that task as a full time job.
- Then delegate, stop or outsource the lowest paying tasks and those where you have only a C or I.

Following this process helps you to focus on doing exactly what you need to grow your company—and love doing it.

Unless you want to start competing on price, starting a race to the bottom that nobody wins, you must understand what is unique about you and how you got where you are. The more easily and clearly you can explain this, the simpler it is for people to buy because they trust you and like who you are.

People buy from people. Outlining the reasons you're different may mean you lose clients to a competitor whose personality or story speaks more strongly to them, but it will also be the reason many people put your product first. Your secret weapon is your ability to demonstrate how you:

---

1   www.cameronherold.com/blog/time-management/8-7-unique

- Have personally achieved the result your clients want and had to struggle and overcome obstacles to get there
- Continually live and breathe the subject of your course and never think you've learnt all there is to know
- Not only know your stuff but have helped others achieve a similar goal, faster and more easily than you did yourself

Not only does this reassure your clients of quality, it also permits you to place a higher value on your time. Should you choose to provide private coaching, consulting or training alongside your product, your clients will recognise you as an expert and be prepared to pay more.

Later I'll show you how to create your expert brand, but for now you need to understand that at least half of the value of your product lies with you, the creator, and your expertise.

What Next? Action Steps

1. Complete the Mapping Realities exercise. What does life 'currently' look like for your potential client? What does life 'ideally' look like for your client having purchased and consumed your product?
2. Think about your expert story. How can you demonstrate your ability to help someone achieve this transformation? What have you had to go through to get where you are today?
3. This is a good point to leave your completed exercise aside, do something different, take some time away and revisit the activity with fresh eyes and renewed energy to make sure you're happy with it. It's a crucial exercise that will help you formulate your marketing.

** BONUS **

To download the Mapping Realities Worksheet my clients use, as discussed in this chapter, and other FREE Bonuses, visit www.DontSleepOnItBook.com/Bonus

Chapter Two

Understanding Your Client

A winning sales strategy doesn't just involve working out how to sell more of what you make. A better plan is to understand what people really value and then to give them exactly that.
—**Bernadette Jiwa**, *Marketing: A Love Story*

What will help you and your product stand out from the competition in a crowded marketplace? And what will build a loyal following of clients who will buy from you again and again? In my experience, it is your ability to give your clients exactly what it is they're looking for and demonstrate your desire to see them succeed.

The reason many expert business owners fail is because they're certain they know what their clients need and they go ahead and build a product without finding out if that assumption is true. They spend time and energy focusing on being better than their competition and put their marketing efforts into saying why they are the best. In other words, it's about the expert, not the people they're there to serve.

Having the best idea, course, success story, event or anything else doesn't automatically make you a winner. In fact, if you *start* by trying to create the best product or service, you never will. A great product starts with having the deepest understanding of your clients' world. If you want to matter to *them*, they have to first matter to you.

This is summed up by Perry Marshall who says in his book *80/20 Sales and Marketing: The Definitive Guide to Working Less and Making More*, 'Selling to the right person is more important than all the sales methods, copywriting techniques, and negotiation tactics in the world. Because the wrong person doesn't have the money. Or the wrong person doesn't care. The wrong person won't be persuaded by anything.'

One of my earliest influences when I began building my first business was Jay Abraham. Jay advocates calling the people who buy your product 'clients'. Normally, there is an invisible line between selling commodities (which have 'customers') and high-value services (which have 'clients'). However, Jay's 'strategy of pre-eminence' suggests that every successful business should think of their buyers as clients, no matter what they sell.

Jay cites Webster's dictionary, which defines a 'client' as 'someone who is under the protection of another'. To think of your customers as clients, no matter how lowly your product, is a transformational mindset. It gives you a duty of care to do what is best for them; you must *increase* the value in your product to ensure they get what they need.

The only way to build a truly meaningful and highly profitable business is to care about your clients in the same the way you care about your own business success.

What Does Knowing Your Client Do for You?

The Mapping Realities exercise in the last chapter helped you paint a picture of your clients' current reality (and a problem they're experiencing) and their aspirations for a life where that problem is no longer there. This exercise teaches us how to build a product that gives the client exactly what they want and need.

But your research into your client doesn't stop there. The more you understand them, the easier it is to create, market and sell courses that get results. What you learn about your clients will help you improve your products, marketing, customer service and sales.

You attract the right people to your business

Many people new to business try to market their product to anyone and everyone who might find it useful. Life coaches are often the worst culprits. Coaching can be adapted to help anyone, and new coaches, not sure where they'd like to direct their efforts or thinking this is unimportant, try to include every possible option in their website and marketing. After all, they're trying to maximise the number of sales and they don't want to alienate particular audience groups or leave anyone out.

However, personalising your content and advertising to the unique preferences of your best clients gives you a much better return on investment. According to eMarketer, 68% of marketers say personalisation based on behavioural data has a high impact on ROI, and 74% say it has a high impact on engagement.[2]

In contrast, taking a scattergun approach not only leaves you with a wishy-washy marketing message (an enormous waste of money), but can also damage your reputation as an expert if the wrong people buy. By 'the wrong people', I mean people who buy on impulse but don't follow through or end up being hard to please. Your success as an expert is closely tied to the results your clients achieve, so the perfect client not only values your course but is so over the moon with the results that they tell everyone they know.

---

2   Econsultancy, April 2013. 'The Realities of Online Personalisation', *Econsultancy*. econsultancy.com/reports/the-realities-of-online-personalisation-report [accessed 12 December 2017]

As a family doctor, Dr Julie Coffey began to see a healthy diet and lifestyle as the most effective way to treat many of the conditions she saw in her surgery every day. Sadly, she soon discovered the vast majority of her patients wanted medication and weren't interested in her advice. Had she insisted on taking this approach, it would have affected their health (and therefore her reputation as a doctor) when they didn't follow through.

Dr Coffey realised that if she wanted to make a difference, she needed to take this information outside the surgery and take it to people who were already motivated to find a new way to manage their health. Now the people who buy her course are ambassadors for Julie's message, making it easier to reach more people.

Knowing your ideal clients, you can direct your marketing budget and efforts towards attracting them into your sales funnel and overcoming their objections so they're more likely to invest and start getting results. This allows you to further refine your course to give even more value, leading to important social proof of your product's success.

You provide a fantastic experience for your clients

When you try to see the world through the eyes of the people you want to matter to, you are at your best. Understanding your clients inevitably leads to better service as your clients become people you enjoy working with and are excited to support.

Great service is big business; companies like Amazon, Apple or Zappos show us that a reputation for looking after your clients does wonders for your bottom line. Apple's 'Genius Bar' customer service model is a large part of the reason the company's retail chain has the highest number of sales per square foot in the US.

In some ways, the world has become more impersonal in the digital age; we communicate via technology and spend time together in a virtual world. Despite this, savvy businesses are becoming more client-focused, not less. With the increase in big data and the amount of algorithms that power our lives (from our Facebook Feeds to our Netflix suggestions) people now expect highly relevant, personalised content wherever they go.

With personalised content as standard, understanding everything there is to know about your client is the only way to stand out. Not only that, once you make your client the hero of the story and show you truly care about their success, your client will begin to care about you.

Defining your client is an ongoing process. Because people and the marketplace are constantly changing, research is essential to not only keep up, but get ahead of the game. In the last decade, the marketplace in nearly every industry has changed drastically, and companies that have not paid careful attention to client behaviour have seen a negative impact on their business. The winners are those that kept up with the trend.

Imagine if Amazon hadn't seen that their clients were slowly taking their shopping away from their desktop computers and towards mobile phones? They may never have created their mobile app. In 2015, *Time* magazine noted that over 70% of holiday shopping on Amazon is now done via mobile devices.[3]

As an entrepreneur, you'll also benefit from observing new behaviours and trends. This inevitably highlights new opportunities, which keeps your business exciting and fun.

Defining your client: where to start

In any marketing 101 course, you'll learn that getting to know your client is the first thing to do, yet an astounding number of businesses move forward with their strategies before truly understanding the type of person they're trying to reach.

---

3   time.com/4162188/amazon-holiday-shopping-statistics-2015

All the tools, forums and books that teach you how to get clear on who you're selling to boil down to one key principle: creating a 'buyer persona', or 'customer avatar'. Your customer avatar is a detailed profile of an ideal client, representing a large segment of your client base. Effective avatars are specific; you'll need one customer avatar for each group of clients for every product you produce.

So how do you gather enough information—and most importantly, the *right* information—to paint a detailed picture of your client?

To start, you'll make assumptions based on what you already know. For example, Micah Lipsmeyer knew from his own experience how hard it is to find a good guitar teacher, and how frustrated he felt when he was still struggling to find the most basic chords. As he improved and started teaching guitar to others, he quickly saw where his students had the most difficulty and listened when they said what wasn't working from them.

Not only did this help Micah become a better teacher, until he was able to make the bold promise of teaching guitar in just ninety days, but it also meant he knew a great deal about his clients when he was ready to market his course.

In addition to these critical observations, you'll need to do some research. Valuable sources of information include:

- **Interviewing your current clients** to find out about their behaviour, interests and needs. Talk to clients who are happy with your product or service, as well as those who aren't happy; both segments will provide valuable insights for your avatar. The interviews also provide the added benefit of making your clients feel heard and appreciated.
- **Analyse your current client database** to know where and how to reach them with your marketing. Pay attention to key trends: how do they discover your content and which channels do they

prefer? For example, do they consume your content through social media on your blog? Do they use desktop computers or mobile phones?

- **Evaluate your current pipeline of prospects**. Listen to your clients in sales conversations to find out what motivates them, and what barriers hold them back from purchasing.
- **Explore a specific demographic.** In addition to your current clients and prospects, there are several easy-to-use online tools to help you gather more insight into potential clients. Facebook Audience Insights and Google Analytics Audience Reports are free tools that give you to the demographic and psychographic makeup of your website and Facebook page visitors.
- **See who buys from your competitors.** In addition to looking at your own website traffic, tools like Compete and SimilarWeb give you a peek into the interests and demographics of your competitors' potential clients.

Most importantly, don't wait until you have everything before creating your customer avatar. Start with what you know and aim to update and continually refine your avatar as you learn more.

Creating your customer avatar

In the *Automated Business System,* our clients use a Customer Avatar Worksheet based on the one recommended by Ryan Deiss, author of *Digital Marketing for Dummies*. Ryan calls the customer avatar 'the Swiss army knife of marketing', which perfectly sums up the many different uses of this single tool.

The sample avatar I'm using here is for one of our main client segments. We've named her 'Freelance Fran'.

Fran's avatar is split into five main sections, each containing vital information that will feed into our product creation, marketing and sales tactics:

- Demographic information
- Goals and values
- Sources of information
- Challenges and pain points
- Objections and role in the purchase process

Your expert model

Demographics make up the core of your customer avatar. This is on the surface information that you can either see, or could find out by asking a couple of questions. Some of it may seem irrelevant, but read through Fran's demographics and you'll already have a pretty clear idea of her life. Knowing her location, education and her home, we can imagine her lifestyle, aspirations, values and any pressures that may affect her business.

Goals and values

Although we can find out more about our clients' aspirations later, we can make a number of assumptions here, because this section reflects the results we offer and the way we like to work. No other client is going to enjoy working with us or get real value from our programme.

Fran is a potential client for the *Automated Business System*, which is ideal for scaling small businesses. Most importantly, we help our clients achieve success through their own means instead of via underhand marketing tactics. We want our clients to share these important values and, obviously, scaling their small business must be a key goal of theirs.

Based on this, we know that Fran's main motivators for working with us are that she wants to win more marketing business and increase her capacity to take on more work. She also values professional development and the use of 'white hat' marketing principles, which are fair and above-board. (White hat marketers abide by the rules and rely on putting plenty of time and effort in, while black hat marketers try to trick search engines and cheat the system.)

Imagine writing a blog post for Fran. We know she wants to increase her business the right way, not through a get-rich-quick scheme, so we may choose a title like 'Five Tried-And-True Marketing Principles to Help You Achieve Success' rather than 'One Speedy Hack to Double your Income in Days'.

Sources of information

Digging deeper into Fran's life, we learn where she gets her information, telling us what she believes in, who she trusts and how she might find out about our programme. Short of asking our real-life Frans directly, much of this will be speculation, but we can also use referral tracking to see which sites our visitors were on when they clicked a link to our site.

As before, some of this information is chosen to reflect the personalities and values of 'gurus' or writers who are in alignment with the *Automated Business System.* If Fran gets her marketing information from Michael Port, who prides himself on his honesty and straightforward approach, she's going to feel at home working with us.

When completing this exercise, it's helpful to make the sources as niche as you possibly can. If we advertised a programme that grew your business to £100,000 in one year on Channel 4, for example, we'd be inundated with interest from people we simply aren't interested in working with. Instead, we dig deeper to send our marketing direct to the people we want to recruit.

To get to the really niche markets, try completing this sentence:

My client gets their information from _____, but no one else does.

Challenges and pain points

Your client's challenges and pain points stand between them and their goal. The more specific they are, the better. Ideally, these are the problems your product or service aims to solve, driving your client to take the positive step of signing up to your course.

One of Fran's main challenges is that she loses business to agencies that offer more services and provide lower-cost work. Because of this, she may be motivated to spend money on a service that allows her to expand her capabilities and win more business.

This is where it becomes imperative to speak to your existing clients to understand their challenges in more detail, or do some research in your target areas if you're starting out. One mistake many rookie marketers make is to assume their clients see things the same way they do; this is rarely the case.

Objections and role in the purchase process

What would cause your client *not* to buy your product or service? Overlook this section at your peril, because when somebody has doubts about purchasing, you need to be prepared.

You'll soon discover your clients' doubts and objections when you start to have sales conversations. If you don't have this kind of conversation, try to talk with people in your ideal client group to find out what concerns they might have about buying your course. You'll be surprised how many people are happy to spend fifteen to twenty minutes talking about themselves! From our sales conversations, we know Fran is conscious of seeing immediate value from the training she invests in. This is a key insight to be aware of so we can emphasise how we help her achieve sales quickly after the training period.

It's also important to identify what role your client plays in the purchase decision. Maybe they're the key decision maker and have the final say, or maybe they're a key influencer. Their role in this process will help determine how you market to them.

Once you've created your customer avatar, you'll have a clear picture of the target market you're selling to. You'll have more insight into what they care about, and how your product can help solve their challenges. You will be able to use this insight to focus, scale and grow your business, to serve more of the right people and get better results.

What next? Action steps

1. There are many reasons why a customer avatar will smooth client relationships and improve your bottom line. Once you're comfortable with your avatar for one of your client segments, build one for each of the other segments of your current or potential audience.

2. It's important to revisit and refine your avatars over time. Consider what further research you can do to get your avatars as accurate as possible.

** FREE BONUS **

To download the Customer Avatar Worksheet discussed in this chapter, and other FREE Bonuses, visit www.DontSleepOnItBook.com/Bonus

PART TWO
LEVERAGING YOUR EXPERTISE

With the business fundamentals in place, it's time to start building a business that puts your skills, experience and knowledge to work on your behalf. In this section of the book, I am going to walk you through the three key things you need to create for your product to fly off the shelves.

I make this sound simple; it's not. Getting this right will require application, thought and hard work, but it can be done! I've seen my clients, starting with nothing more than an idea, write, record and launch valuable course content that attracts plenty of interest and sales.

The first thing you'll learn is how to create an expert brand—distinguishing yourself from the competition based on your personality and values, and a unique 'expert model' that describes the process you use to achieve consistent results. You'll learn that a strong brand helps your clients trust you, therefore increasing the chances of a sale.

Next, I'll walk you through the process of creating a course based on your expert model and your understanding of your clients' journey, and structured to help them take small and manageable steps towards the promised result.

Finally, you'll learn about sales funnels, which lead your client towards the point of sale, building trust so when they arrive, the purchase decision has already been made. You've made the sale—now you need to deliver the content.

Chapter Three

Creating Your Expert Brand

A brand is not just a logo, it's the overall impression you give to your audience and customers. Your brand expresses the value you provide. It's you!

—Amy Locurto

I n Part One of this book, you learned that a leveraged business succeeds by rejecting the money-for-time business model in favour of hands-off products that create a consistent, desirable result. Secondly, you discovered how your client is the linchpin of your business. The more in-depth information you collect about them—from basic demographics through to their role in the purchase process—the easier it is to create, market and sell products that make a significant difference to their lives.

However, although both principles are driven by client information, the best clients for your business will be attracted to who you are and the unique difference you can make to their world. That is what truly resonates with people and compels them to part with their hard-earned cash. (Not surprisingly, the first consulting session a new *Automated Business System* client goes through with us is a detailed exploration of what makes them truly different and how and where they really stand out.)

Expert branding is the process of establishing yourself as the expert changemaker your clients have been looking for to give them the knowledge, skills and support they desperately need.

What is a brand?

Before we dive into defining your brand, it's important to define what 'branding' means. This word is overused and often misunderstood.

When many people speak of branding, they mean the visual appearance of a company or product—their logo, colours and fonts. This isn't completely wrong, because these elements are carefully considered and used strategically as a visual shortcut to the person or product they represent. Some brands are so recognisable that marketers can play with the visual elements and still be sure of creating a connection in the audience's mind.

Unfortunately, this leads people to believe that creating a brand is as easy as getting a logo design from Fiverr and making sure they use it on everything they do.

This isn't true.

However important these elements are, they are only the visual representation of the *actual* brand. As such, they come much later in the branding process because they must tell the entire story of the values, vision and personality of the company or individual behind the product. David A. Aaker clarifies this in his book *Branding: 20 Principles That Drive Success* by saying, 'A brand vision should attempt to go beyond functional benefits to consider organizational values; a higher purpose; brand personality; and emotional, social, and self-expressive benefits.'

Creating a brand is not a one-time affair. Your brand lays the foundation for a long-term relationship with your client, which will succeed or fail based on whether your products and behaviour deliver what your clients have been led to expect. If you fail to live up to the values you profess to represent, your brand will fail.

Your expert brand

Branding has become a buzzword in the overcrowded online marketplace because so much information is available and so many products and services look the same. How do clients know which is best and which ones can they trust? How can you justify charging higher than the market rate?

When selling a product based on your expertise, clients must know and trust *you* (the expert). In the *Automated Business System*, we work with our clients to build a brand grounded in:

- **Authenticity:** Their personality, purpose and values
- **Expertise:** Their education and experience, social proof and client results
- **Expert model**: The unique process they use to achieve specific results

Authenticity

Imagine meeting someone for the first time. When you meet, you each make assumptions about the other person, based on how they look, what they say and how they behave. With little information to go on, you make a decision whether this is your kind of person or not.

As the relationship continues, you learn more about this person, but you already have certain notions and expectations. As humans, we create an emotional attachment to our first impressions, which can be hard to let go of.

A similar thing happens when prospects meet a digital brand. This brand has a personality, purpose and values which are attractive to the right client group. If the client's experience doesn't live up to that expectation, the client will be disappointed and leave (probably leaving very public negative feedback behind).

The only way to manage this is to work from your passions and live and breathe the principles you teach. It doesn't work to chase a lucrative market if you've no interest in the subject. As the founder of Amazon, Jeff Bezos, said, 'One of the huge mistakes people make is that they try to force an interest on themselves. You don't choose your passions; your passions choose you.'

Many years ago, I learnt this the hard way, when I spent six months researching and writing a book on the secrets of raising happy and healthy hamsters. I sold one $47 download. It was a sobering lesson: without a passion for your subject, your business won't work.

In contrast, I spent years testing and refining my business model until the *Automated Business System* was born. This programme was the result of my passion and determination to not only teach people how to build a successful online business, but also put the systems in place to ensure they succeed. As a business, we live our values, using the same marketing principles I teach my clients. This has helped over 150 experts and changemakers trust me to help them leverage their business and have more impact with their expertise.

Expertise

Inevitably, what follows passion is expertise—a deep understanding of your topic and clear evidence that you have a process that works.

Your expertise adds value to your brand because it helps to differentiate you from the many similar products in your niche and reassures the client that your products will deliver results.

Amazon is full of how-to books on anything from marketing to training your dog. The author may or may not know anything about the subject (many haven't written the book at all!) and it's dubious whether there is any value in the content. Far too many are churned out and sold for pennies in the hope of making a few bucks from impulse buys.

To set your product apart, you need to provide evidence of your expertise. Branding yourself as an expert starts on your landing pages, with evidence of your training, qualifications and experience in the field. Experts demonstrate their results with the help of client testimonials and associations with famous names or known and trusted brands.

For example, Micah Lipsmeyer demonstrates his expertise on his website by sharing his journey from awkward beginner to successful performer and accomplished guitar teacher. He lists well-known groups he has performed with and lets his client stories speak for his ability to teach.

And Emma Teggarty and her business partner James Crew help people turn a passion for health and fitness into a profitable personal trainer business. To show they're the right team for the job, they focus on credentials. Their 'about' page is far shorter than Micah's but is packed with information about their achievements in the fields of business and sport.

Another example is that of the leading medical team in the UK which has delivered over 3,000 babies to date. They founded YourPregnancyDoctor.com, which acts as a learning resource for women hoping to get pregnant or who are already pregnant. The website contains over 450 freely-available articles, and also offers video courses for purchase. (This website is only open to the UK market.)

In all three cases, they reinforce their expert brand through content, results and happy clients, giving prospects free guidance towards achieving their goal. Micah demonstrates his teaching abilities by regularly sharing new guitar-playing tips while Emma and James discuss business building strategies for fitness professionals on their blog and social media.

Your expert model

The final element of your expert brand is what we describe in the *Automated Business System* as your Expert Model. This is a visual representation of the process your clients experience on the journey towards their goal, and is an indispensable reference point for your work.

The expert model is a valuable asset to your business because it turns information in the public domain into your intellectual property. None of the information in the expert model for the *Automated Business System* is in any way unique, but as the model represents the exact process we use to get our clients results, we can claim ownership of a system that isn't used anywhere else.

As long as this is an honest depiction of your own teaching process, it's a perfectly valid way of adding credibility to your brand. The expert model demonstrates that you've thought about, planned, structured and tested your content until you have a solution that works.

How the expert model works

This is the *Automated Business System* expert model. Looking at it, you can see each stage of the process our clients go through while building their business, and how we have grouped them into three main stages which we visit as their journey progresses.

The first stage of the programme focuses on strategy, starting with the client's vision for their business, through to defining the online course product and the sales funnel processes through which the business will be run. We know the business strategy is essential for creating an effective business and we don't implement anything until the entire strategy is clearly defined.

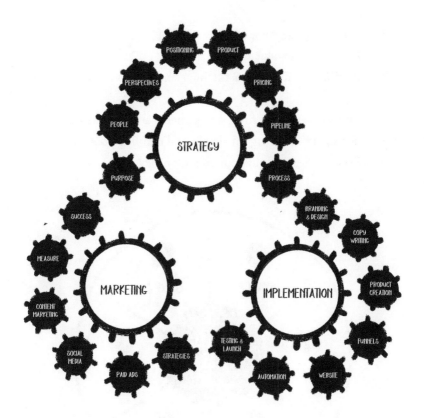

The next stage is implementation. This involves branding, copywriting, product creation, filming, and the build and complete automation of the entire sales process. In the final section of the programme, we teach the client to choose, implement and test marketing strategies to reach the final element—results.

Our clients' models aren't always as complex as this, but they don't have to be. They must simply illustrate each important stage or element of the process they use to get results.

Deborah Fielding helps speakers and celebrities build a successful speaking business with more bookings and higher fees. Her model is based on the aptly-named acronym SPEAKS, standing for:

- **Source**—you, the speaker
- **Power**—your value to paying clients
- **Emphasis**—five key marketing elements, and how to get them right
- **Attract**—where to find paying clients and how to get signed
- **'Kontract'**—nailing the details and defining your fee
- **Service**—setting out your client journey

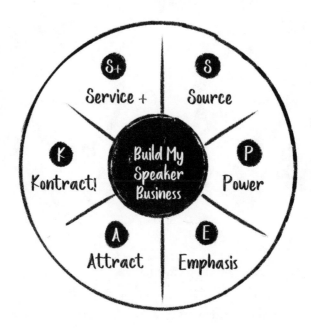

As with any well-constructed model, this clearly illustrates the value of working with Deborah by showing what clients will learn, defining the scope of her work (speaker training is not included) and demonstrating the extent of her expertise. When introducing her model, Deborah expands on each element to reveal the different subjects that make them up.

Further uses of your expert model

In addition to being an essential element of your expert brand, the expert model feeds into your business strategy and product implementation in a number of ways:

It can be repurposed into different products and content. Once the expert model has been established, it is your signature system. But it also provides a rich source of ideas for further products and endless content on its main themes.

It reminds you of what's important: Many entrepreneurs fall victim to 'shiny object syndrome' (oh, look—a penny!), becoming attracted or disheartened by the appearance of a new training system they feel they need to incorporate into their portfolio. The expert model keeps the focus on what's already working (and what your clients expect).

It helps you attract the right clients: With the expert model, you can lay out the prerequisites for client success. As you can see from the *Automated Business System* model, idea generation isn't part of what we do, so we expect our clients to have their own area of expertise.

With a model, you can deter people who aren't ready for your course or, if your course teaches absolute beginners, you can avoid disappointing prospects who have advanced skills. This has the advantage of recruiting those who will get most value from your product, leading to fewer disappointed clients and more rave reviews.

It's easy to remember: The model can be broken down into a simple checklist to ensure you do everything in the correct order and nothing is missed out. When speaking, it's easy to break down what you help people with and the results you achieve.

It's easy to track your progress: When the client has enrolled on the programme, they can easily follow the process and track their progress, helping them see results quickly and feel a sense of achievement early on.

It's easy for prospects to understand: Having a model is ideal for your marketing. Your clients can easily see what is included in the package, and you can break down what each of the stages or modules achieves on the route towards their goal.

It's easy to commit into practice: A good expert model clearly lays out a set of simple modules in an easy-to-follow structure. Even when they have finished your course, clients can return to the model time and again.

Carve out a space in people's minds

Ideally, your expert brand provides the perfect partnership between your expertise and what your clients need. It serves to reassure your ideal clients that you can deliver on your promises (both in terms of results and the values you adhere to in your work) and gives you clarity and confidence to set bold and inspiring goals for your clients to achieve.

Once you have defined your brand, the real work begins. Hiten Shah, founder of Kissmetrics, says in his blog, 'You build a brand when you've carved out a piece of people's brains,'[4] meaning when there is a need for your area of expertise, people think of you and not your competitors. This takes both persistence and time, as well as patience and long-term thinking.

Hiten believes a successful personal brand requires novelty (which the steps in this chapter are designed to create) and repetition. On the whole, people are more amenable towards thinking of *you*, when you demonstrate you're thinking of *them*, but you can't just do this one time.

---

4   hitenism.com/build-brand

Repetition—by giving your clients a consistently positive experience, telling similar stories, repeatedly giving valuable advice—creates familiarity at first, then believability, then trust in your brand.

Marketers use terms such as 'effective frequency' to define the ideal number of times a person needs to hear a message before they buy a product, but this is missing the point. If you can successfully create a space for your brand in people's minds, they're likely to stay with you for the long term, not just buy a product and move on.

What next? Action steps

- Use your 'mapping realities' exercise as the starting point for your own expert model. List the steps necessary to take your clients from their current reality to their ideal reality. Write down everything you think they may need to learn or do.

- Consider how to group these steps into categories or themes to create a concise model that's easy to follow and remember.

Chapter Four

Creating Your Course
(or Other Online Product)

First of all, we really need to care about the people we are designing for, understand what their dreams and desires and priorities are, and then we have to use that understanding as the driving force of the work we put forward, because the second we know what questions… are important, then all we have to do is answer them.
—**Bjarke Ingels**, Architect

I t is only when you understand both your clients' and your own value that you can create a life-changing course. We might believe we have the ability to create the perfect programme on our own, but the reality is we're not the ones who get to decide. It is humbling to know that the people we serve decide what's worthy and what's not.

But to create the perfect product—the one that really makes a difference in your clients' lives—you have to also understand the difference *you* bring to your line of work. You need to understand where your skills, experience and expertise make the most difference in people's lives and where you fit into their journey. The perfect solution stems from where your unique abilities meet your clients' desires.

Your expert model therefore provides the perfect basis for a life-changing course because it describes the main areas of your expertise, and how they work together to achieve the perfect outcome for your clients. It provides a clear structure (a starting point, an end point and the steps in between) that can be put to immediate use in your course. Verne Harnish explains this well in his book *Scaling Up: How a Few Companies Make It... and Why the Rest Don't* saying, 'You don't have a real strategy if it doesn't pass two tests: First, what you're planning to do really matters to enough customers; and second, it differentiates you from your competition.'

As the expert changemaker, you must focus on helping your clients overcome their struggle by leading them towards your vision of what success looks like for them. In this chapter, you'll learn how to plan and produce an online course based on a transformational client journey, from struggle to success.

The path to transformation

Earlier in the book, I described how a leveraged business sells outcomes, not time. This allows you to serve more people while stepping away from the wheel.

When you start to define a course, you have to consider not just the outcome but also where you client is in relation to achieving that goal. Ideally, they will have a strong emotional connection to the outcome but can't see how to get there. A course becomes extremely valuable if it provides a transformation—a move from one reality to the next—that your clients don't know how achieve.

You already described this transformation in the Mapping Realities exercise, where you visualised your client's current and ideal realities. Your expert model describes the stages of your client's journey from one to the other, and forms the basis for your course and the content you create to lead clients to a purchase decision.

In the case of Deborah Fielding, who created the SPEAKS expert model I described in Chapter Three, her clients are accomplished speakers who either work for free or who charge a fee but aren't getting work. Deborah's model takes them from this frustrating situation to a reality where they are regularly booked for paid speaking engagements.

The six stages of her model take her clients on a journey from one reality to the next. Her course helps them know and express their value, set up their promotional funnel, find the right engagements, lock in a fee and provide great service to attract repeat bookings and positive reviews. With all elements in place, they should experience a dramatic upturn in their business fortunes, thus completing the transformation.

Similarly, YourPregnancyDoctor.com offers four video courses which walk mums-to-be through the different stages of pregnancy, starting with when they first find out they are (or might be) pregnant. The videos address all the questions they're likely to ask at each stage and provide them with all the information they'll need as their pregnancy progresses. They provide practical pregnancy and parenting advice from a team of health experts, with lifetime access to the videos so they can refresh their knowledge for any future pregnancies. It's all too easy for women to forget to ask questions in busy antenatal clinics, and it can be hard to absorb and understand all the information they're given. Dr Keith's years of experience have taught him what pregnant women want and need to know, all of which is addressed in this course. By following the course, pregnant women can ensure that they're happy, healthy and comfortable throughout their pregnancy and beyond.

If your course focuses on one area of your model, the same principle applies: you must define the problem the course addresses, the ideal outcome taking the course would achieve and the elements your student needs for the transformation to take place.

Creating your course structure

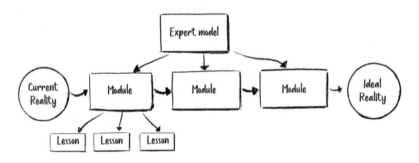

Planning a course based on your expert model is relatively simple, but it must be well structured to make sure the elements are taught in the right order and complex concepts are broken down into easy-to-understand chunks.

Level One–Modules

I recommend splitting your courses into modules covering the key stages of your client's learning. The most obvious way to define your modules is to create one for each main section of your expert model. In Deborah Fielding's case, there would be six modules covering source, power, emphasis, attract, 'kontract' and service. You can think of the modules as milestones on your student's journey; completion of each module brings them one step closer to their ideal reality.

You will need to define the outcomes, or goals, for each module. The same as creating an overarching goal for your course, each stage must have clearly defined outcomes. This allows students to know what they are aiming for and track their progress through the course. Marking off a series of small achievements is a strong motivator and helps build confidence in a new skill.

Level Two–Lessons

Each module consists of one or more lessons, once again defined with clear learning outcomes that help you structure your content and give your students something to aim for.

It is important to keep your course materials and exercises incredibly doable. The more you can break things down and keep people focused on step-by-step micro-actions, the easier it is for them to experience success, which keeps them motivated and ready to learn. Therefore, each lesson needs to cover a single subject area so your client can learn and succeed at one thing at a time.

The combination of the lessons in a module is everything students need to achieve the module's goal. For example, Deborah Fielding's 'Emphasis' module focuses on the different promotional tools a successful

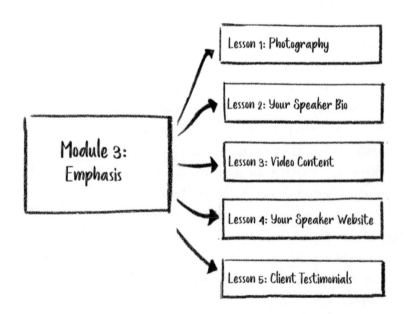

speaker needs to build their business. Her lessons might include one each on photographs, speaker biographies, video content, the speaker's website and client testimonials.

Order of delivery

It's important you present the modules, and the lessons within a module, in a logical order. For example, if you were Tim Harper, teaching students to ski, would you teach them advanced carving skills if they couldn't parallel ski? Of course not. It is essential to include all the necessary modules, but the order of your teaching also has a direct impact on your clients' success.

In the *Automated Business System* model, we have three groups of elements which must be in place in the correct order to move people smoothly towards their goal: strategy, implementation and marketing. We know that if our students go straight to implementation without a strategy in place, the product and the business are unlikely to work. It's also logical to have the entire business model in place before marketing. Otherwise, clients may reach an unfinished website or want to buy a course that's not ready to sell.

Creating lessons

With your course structured into modules and lessons, and a logical order worked out, it's time to create each of the lessons that make up your course.

Once you understand the format for a lesson, it's relatively straightforward to create them all. Each lesson should contain the following elements:

- **Learning outcomes**: what the student should know and/or be able to do once the lesson is complete

- **Teaching**: explaining or demonstrating what the student needs to know
- **Activity**: to embed the learning so your students don't just hear or read the information, then forget

Learning outcomes

The first and most important stage in lesson creation is defining the learning outcomes, so your lesson lays out a clear path towards a specific skill or area of knowledge. This gives you and your student clarity, so you know you're on track and they can clearly see what they've achieved.

Learning outcomes are best defined with a verb, such as 'know', 'write' or 'understand'. For example, if we were to take one of the five areas of communication in the 'emphasis' stage of Deborah Fielding's speaker business course, the learning outcomes may look like this:

Module: 3—Emphasis

Lesson Title: Client testimonials

Learning outcomes: On completion of this lesson, the student should be able to:

Know what a really powerful client testimonial looks like

Write a testimonial request that's easy for the client to complete

Turn the client response into a powerful testimonial

Use the testimonial for maximum impact on their website and other marketing outlets

---

The more you can tie your course back to participants' lives, the easier it is to keep them interested and engaged. Remind them why they're there, and you'll not only see improved interest levels but also stronger performance, especially among those who doubt their abilities. For this reason, each learning outcome should describe an element of the client's ideal reality—bringing them one step closer to their goal.

Teaching

As the expert, you know what to teach to get the right outcomes, but when delivering the content, it's important to consider which format to deliver it in. Educational theory suggests that your students may have a preference, finding it easier to learn from one of four different teaching formats.

The idea of individual learning styles has been around since the 1970s. This theory suggests people absorb information more effectively if it is delivered to fit their preferred learning style. The four main learning styles are visual, auditory, read/write and kinaesthetic.

Visual	Auditory
Visual learners prefer images, maps and graphical representations of content. They remember information visually, seeing it as pictures in their mind.	These learners learn through listening and speaking. They may embed learning through discussion, repetition or mnemonic devices.
Read/write	**Kinaesthetic**
People with this preference learn through words. They might like to take copious notes and absorb written information better than that presented in a video or audio presentation.	Kinaesthetic students love tactile information and prefer to learn through doing. This means they are most likely to remember information if they are given a task and have to work through it themselves.

Not everybody agrees it's necessary to adapt teaching to suit each individual student (fortunately for the creation of an online course!) but the common educational practice of covering all bases makes sense. Each additional method of presenting the information presents another way for students to learn. Most popular courses on the Internet today will offer you a combination of video and PDF worksheets.

A good example of combining different methods is Healthletix's personal training programme created by Tony Thompson and Matt Nelson (healthletix.co). The programme is made up of multiple learning styles. There are nine videos that show specific fitness routines and workouts, as well as nine cooking demonstrations, filmed in Tony's kitchen where he walks you through the ingredients and cooks it in front of you. All the recipes are provided in recipe sheets too, for easy reference. When it comes to your fitness workout, you have access to an app called the 'Healthletix Timer' to give you support. And based on your selected plan, you'll get a personalised meal and workout plan written for you for one, two and four weeks respectively.

Arvind Devalia's *Ultimate Life Transformation System* also uses a variety of styles. Arvind is a life coach and the best-selling author of *Get The Life You Love* who runs a popular blog with 4,000+ readers at ArvindDevalia.com/blog and a Facebook page with 29,000 fans at the time of writing. Based on his experience of coaching high achievers working in the city, he has created a six month programme that offers one sixty minute call each month, a half day consult to start, and webinar training delivered once a month online where Arvind runs a presentation, using PowerPoint slides with his voice over.

And Norva Abiona combines video lessons along with worksheets in her seven-module programme *Rise of the Warrior Queen*, which supports women who want to overcome their challenges and embrace their inner and outer warrior.

As part of the *Automated Business System,* we suggest our clients combine videos with written worksheets. The videos accommodate visual and auditory learners (with the help of slides visualising certain contexts, not just talking heads), while written information is useful for people who prefer the read/write style. Adding activities to a worksheet helps embed the learning kinaesthetically by asking the students to put their learning into practice.

Activity

With your teaching delivered by video (and possibly with written support), the final element is to set one or more activities that get students to engage with difficult concepts and put their learning into practice. An effective approach is to insert a single activity for each lesson—remember, one small step at a time!

The two most effective activities to include are a quiz to ensure they've remembered correctly and fill-in-the-blank worksheets to complete while the video is in progress, or tasks to carry out once the lesson is complete. Both these elements also help increase the perceived value of your online course and you can use a tool like Canva.com to design and put them together.

Without setting any kind of activity, your students may take a listen-and-run approach to their learning and walk away having learnt little, if anything, that will change their circumstances. If you want to maximise the impact of your work on your participants' lives, it's not enough for them to just consume your content. Even if every word is valuable and useful, nobody gets results unless they take action towards their goal.

Setting activities also allows you to confidently offer a money-back guarantee, because you can ask students to provide evidence they've taken the action you know is needed to get good results. If you've written your course well, you will have directed them towards a positive outcome and will get few, if any, complaints!

Another way to deliver the Activity element would be to include access to a community area, like a private Facebook Group for buyers only. You could offer this as a space for them to engage with other clients, ask questions, provide responses to others and stay connected to you.

Once you have decided how you will present your content, then it's time to look at the nitty-gritty details of each one.

Naming your course

At some stage you will have to choose a name for your course. This isn't something you should do in a hurry. The title will often determine whether people take an interest or move on.

It's best to wait until the course is completed before you decide what to call it. Often, the course itself will suggest a title. You may run through several possibilities. If you aren't sure which to choose, testing them through a survey or focus group can be helpful.

Titles that are to the point and powerful allow people to decide immediately if your course will offer what they're looking for. Being clear doesn't mean you need to be dull, however. If possible, you should seek to generate excitement and interest with your title.

It's worth researching other similar course to see which titles are selling well. That will give you an idea of the type of title that appeals to your particular market. The following tips will help you make your choice:

- **Keep it short:** A short title is easier to remember. You can use a subtitle to carry more of your message. A two-part name will be clear but still allow space to expand on your topic. Your title should be as descriptive as possible without being verbose.
- **Clearly convey the benefits:** Including outcomes into your course name gives you a results-oriented title that reminds potential customers about their problem and presents a solution. Your title should make a promise as a clear opportunity.
- **Choose clarity over cleverness:** If your title can be understood in different ways, it might attract the wrong audience. It can also create confusion and put people off buying. The title

should first and foremost be informative and make it clear what the content is about.

- **Specify your audience:** Think about who is likely to buy your course. Writing for different groups might require a different choice of words, tone and style. If you're producing a course that will only appeal to a limited group, use a title that will reflect this. For example, if you are wiring for a particular professional group, you can use industry terms and jargon. You might also want to indicate the level of your course—whether it's aimed towards beginners or someone more advanced.

- **Say it aloud:** Words that sound good together are more memorable and more likely to trigger interest. Also, a title that sounds different from others suggests the content will also be interesting.

- **Use naming unity:** If you're offering a course series or related courses, use a common name format.

Creating content slides

Slides are a straightforward way of presenting your information. They work well as stand-alone content, or you can use them to supplement videos or other course content. For example, you could choose to combine your slides with video content by flipping through them while talking over them with screenflow. That gives you the option of having a video of you appear in the bottom right hand corner of your slides.

Your slides don't need to be fancy and complicated. On the contrary, the best ones are simple and easy to follow. Like Garr Reynolds says in his book *Presentation Zen: Simple Ideas on Presentation Design and Delivery,* 'When you look at your slide, notice where your eye is drawn first, second, and so on. What path does your eye take?'

However, that doesn't mean you don't want them to look good. Keep to the point! Don't put endless paragraphs on information on your slides. If you need to give a lot of text, it should appear in an ebook or other downloadable file. Slides are best for bullet points, very short sentences or graphics. If you need to go into detail about a point, break it down and use multiple slides.

Colour

A simple way of making your slides look better is through using colour effectively. If you already have a brand colour, the choice will be easier. It's important that your course has the same look and feel as the rest of your content and using colour will help you achieve that. Make sure that any additional colours you use harmonise rather than clash with your main colour.

People attach meanings to colours and colour combinations without realising it. For example, red represents danger and blue is business-like. Yellow and black together grab attention but can make people feel uncomfortable as this combination is often used as a warning. If you use yellow and black together for titles, people will feel like you're shouting at them.

It's easiest if you stick to one main colour and one or two complementary colours. For example, you could choose one dark and one light colour to use together and a third colour for shapes or other design elements.

Some colours look great together—and others don't. But it isn't as simple as saying this colour goes with that one. A lot depends on context. If you had a bar chart with a dark background and dark bars, no-one would be able to read it. You need to colours to contrast in some way. There are plenty of online colour generators that can help you choose a colour scheme, and PowerPoint and Keynote have colour scheme pre-sets that you can use as starting points, but if you understand how colours work together, you can create your own.

There are logical and simple to follow rules for creating colour schemes that work by using the colour wheel. (If you take a look at a colour wheel online, you'll be able to see how this works.) For example, you can use colours that are next to each other on the wheel if you want a soft, less contrasting design. Or you might choose to use colours that are opposite each other for higher contrast.

Whatever colour scheme you choose, it should suit the needs of your graphic or slide. Simply ask yourself, 'What is the goal of this slide?' and you can work out how much (or how little) contrast you need.

Online colour schemes that can help you out include:

- Colour Lovers: (colourlovers.com): With this palette generator you can search for colours by keyword or hex code. However, the quality of the palettes is variable so you need to be discerning.
- Coolors (coolors.co): This is very easy to use. You can simply use your space bar to generate palettes or type in the hex code and lock it so it doesn't change and then press the spacebar and it'll generate palettes that go with that colour.
- Adobe (color.adobe.com): You can either start with a specific colour you want to use and generate hues that look good with it or play with the wheel and see what comes up.

When you're choosing colours for your course, think about how you want to be perceived. You can draw inspiration from your favourite brands. The colours you choose for your slides can be used as solid background colours, in shapes or other design elements on the slide.

It's best to avoid a completely white background on a slide as it can be glaring. Tone it down by using a soft colour that will be easy on the eyes. Dark backgrounds can be effective but take more care when combining with images.

Whatever colour scheme you choose in the end, the important thing is to be consistent.

Text

Ideally, you should have no more than three lines of text on a slide and no more than six words per line. Limit punctuation to the bare minimum as it can needlessly clutter the slide. NEVER type in all caps as it's difficult to read and is like SHOUTING at your audience.

Fonts

There are two types of font—serif and sans serif. Serif fonts are those with small embellishments at the end of the strokes while sans serif fonts have no such enhancement.

Times New Roman is a serif font
Arial is a sans serif font

In general, sans serif fonts, like Arial and Open Sans, are easier to read on a screen, although you might choose a serif font for headings.

To avoid being distracting, it's best to use a common font such as Helvetica or Arial. Although plenty of free fonts are available on the internet, many of these don't have the full set of characters—something you might not discover until you want to use something that isn't there! Also, many use obliques rather than true italics. This has the effect of making you realise something isn't quite right although you can't put your finger on what it is. And don't use more than two fonts—one for headings and one for content—or your slide will look messy.

Make sure that whatever font you choose is large enough to read easily. However, that doesn't mean you should use the biggest size that will fit on your slide. If your text is too squashed, it won't be clear. Also, remember that some fonts take up more space than others, so although a certain point size might look perfect on slides with one font, you may have to adjust the size if you use a different font.

Images

Images can often say far more than words. A picture aids in memory by making a visual connection to an abstract idea. Memory rests on connections and a vivid picture forms a solid connection.

The best images to use are ones you supply yourself. You can guarantee they will be 100% original and safe to use. However, if you aren't a dab hand with a camera, you might want to download a suitable image from the internet. Some good sites for free to use images include:

- Pixabay
- StockSnap
- Pexels
- Unsplash
- DepositPhotos

It's likely that you will want to use text with your images. If the image is dark in colour, you can use white as your text colour. If white doesn't look good, experiment with another light colour. Conversely, if the image is light, you will need to use dark coloured text.

You can add text directly onto a busy image by creating a coloured shape and then pasting the text inside it. When doing this, make sure to add the text in its own text box so you have more control over the formatting.

As with any design, cut the clutter. No more than one graphic image or chart per slide is a good rule (excluding any logo or other recurring element in the design).

Finally, the rule to remember in slide design is the 6-6-6 rule: no more than 6 words per bullet, 6 bullets per image, and 6 word slides in a row.

Filming

Obviously, you'll want the best quality footage for your course that you can manage. However, if you browse through YouTube and watch some of the videos that have gone viral, you'll notice that many of them are of low technical quality.

Unless you're experienced at making videos, your first step should be to watch other people's content. Check out any that teach something online. Even bad ones can teach you something. It can help to watch a video about a subject you're not interested in—that will allow you to better focus on the techniques used.

Your videos don't need to be very long. It's better to have several short and focused videos rather than one that goes on… and on… and on…

Shooting high quality videos can boost the perceived value of your course, but that comes second to good information that's well presented. Before spending any serious money on equipment, check out what you already own. A laptop, a simple camera (even on your tablet or smartphone) is enough to get started with.

The most important thing is to make sure your camera is stable. A selfie stick that clamps the device to a table can be sufficient. Even better is a small tripod.

Good lighting makes all the difference. If possible, shoot in natural light. That often means scheduling filming for early in the day. If you're shooting indoors, use a room with a large window so you can take advantage of the light. However, don't place yourself (or whoever you're shooting) directly in front of the window. If you do that, you'll simply look like a dark silhouette. Instead, sit *opposite* the window.

Adding a small light to your camera won't cost much but could improve the quality of your shoot. If you can afford to invest a little more, you could consider buying a ring-light and position it nearby. Should you invest in a better quality camera, it's probably worth your while to buy more lights—especially if you're going to make regular videos. For example, you could use one on the right and left in front of you and one on the wall behind you.

However, if you're going to spend money on one piece of equipment, it should probably be your microphone. Before beginning to speak, capture a minute or so of the base sound of the room by simply turning on your mic and letting it record. You can use this sound later if you need to fill an audio gap or smooth out a transition. Also, if you're recording sound and video separately, you will have to line them up at the editing stage. The easiest way to facilitate this is to clap at the start of your video to produce a large waveform that can be easily visually identified. Similarly, if you make a mistake that you plan to cut out, make an audible sound that will appear in the waveforms.

You can only spend so long sorting out your equipment—at some point you'll have to get in front of the camera. The trick to doing it well is to practice. You can make life much easier by remembering to create silent lead time between your takes and after you make a mistake.

Wear something that makes you feel good and reflects your brand. A smart suit will look good if you're trying to be business-like, while a t-shirt and jeans is better if you want a friendly, informal approach. Try to avoid wearing all white or black, too many patterns, small checks, large prints or loud colours. (The same goes for fussy jewellery; it's distracting). It's best to wear safe colours like dark blues—darker colours tend to look better on camera. However, the important thing is that you feel good about yourself—it can help to dress just a little bit smarter than you think you need to.

Have a drink of water before you begin—the last thing you want is a coughing fit. Sit up straight and take a deep breath before you start. If you slump, it will look like you're not really interested in what you're saying. Keep any nervous fidgets under control. You might not be aware of how you constantly tap your fingers when you're talking, but it could drive your viewers mad. Doing a practice run and reviewing it will help you spot any habits like this and think of how to control them. That might mean having something in your hands to fiddle with off-camera, in this case.

Where you position yourself depends on how you're preparing your video. If it's going to include text on screen, you will need to sit to one side. Otherwise, you will want to place yourself in the centre of the screen. Starting with a smile makes you look sincere and confident. Grinning manically might fascinate viewers, but in completely the wrong way. Look directly at the camera as if it's your friend. It's less intimidating if you speak to the camera as if it's one person rather than worry about the hundreds who could watch your video.

At first you're likely to feel uncomfortable, and might speak faster than usual due to nerves. Don't rush. People need to understand what you're saying so you actually need to speak a little more slowly than you would in normal conversation. Slowing down will also help you to avoid too many ummms and aaahs.

It might sound obvious, but make sure you're completely familiar with your planned content. If your presentation is very detailed, a teleprompter can be useful (for example, you can download a teleprompter app if you have an iPad) . Alternatively, you could have a large piece of paper pasted up in front of you but out of sight of the camera. It isn't necessary to read from it word for word—a brief list of points may be all you need to keep you on track. Even if you're one of those lucky people who can memorise a script easily, you might still find it helpful to have this list available, just in case you dry up.

Don't put on a more important-sounding voice. It's best to use your natural voice—your video should reflect who you are, rather than someone you might like to be.

If you do make a mistake, either carry on or pause for a moment and then repeat what you messed up. You can deal with that on your edit. Similarly, if you can't stop yourself from wriggling or talking too fast, it might be time for a break. Remember, everyone makes mistakes and there's nothing wrong with doing another take.

Once you've finished recording, you'll need to edit your video. If you use a PC, Movie Maker is a free option. If you're on Mac, iMovie is free. You can also get video editing apps on your smartphone. If you're going into record yourself in combination with slides, OC users should go for Camtasia (a free trial is available) while Mac users can use ScreenFlow. For professional level videos, you'll need Adobe Premier Pro or Final Cut Pro.

Screencasts are often used in course creation. They record what's happening on your screen, if you are creating how-to videos or demonstrations, which are essential for some courses. Camastia or ScreenFlow are two highly recommended tools, ideal for producing screencasts.

Adding further benefits to enhance your course

Every course on its own should be created to deliver the outcome you have promised. This is an unbreakable rule. However, there could be additional benefits you could offer to enhance the course, such as a weekly Q&A webinar, one-to-one time for coaching, consulting, teaching or mentoring, interviews with industry experts, and even offering to review or critique work based on the industry you might be in.

The idea isn't to bulk up your course or make it look larger than it needs to be. Remember, the more elements you package into your course, the more work you'll have to do on an ongoing basis. Not to mention that it might not even be useful to the client. The trick is to always question how anything you wish to add will help your client achieve their outcome. Does it move them to the outcome quicker than if you didn't have it? If it does not affect, don't include it.

Once you have decided the core elements of your course (your modules and lessons) and the format you wish to deliver it through, it's important to write this down into a single document or spreadsheet for easy reference while you go about building it.

It's also important to give yourself the day off and leave this to the side. Take some time away from it. Do something different. Rest your mind. Sleep on it, and come back with fresh eyes tomorrow. This way you'll be able to assess whether you've missed anything critical and put it into the course.

Putting your courses online

One of the goals of your leveraged business is to deliver your courses without having to be there, and still serve far more people than you would if you ran in-person courses every week.

What I discovered with my first automated business was the amazing phenomenon of making sales while I was on holiday (or asleep!) and this still doesn't get tired. An automated course sits in cyberspace, set up to deliver your modules, worksheets and activities as you designed them to be delivered, in the order they're meant to be received.

These days, you don't have to be a tech genius to set up a client-friendly online course. As online learning becomes ever-more popular, multiple learning platforms are becoming available that make it simple to upload your content and turn it into an attractive, well-structured course.

My current favourite platform is Teachable.com, which is robust, flexible and really simple to use but there are plenty of other options available. When deciding which platform to choose, don't just go for what's free or really cheap. A poor client experience will count against your brand! You may wish to consider:

- How easy it is to upload and structure your content
- Which other features (such as quizzes or downloads) can be added
- The different payment options you can offer clients
- Whether you can offer course bundles, or a tiered course structure (such as silver, gold and platinum versions of the same course)
- Whether you can upload the courses onto your own domain
- What kind of support you will receive

The hard work you've done on your client research and expert model provides the perfect foundation for a course that will give your clients great results. With the key stages of your client transformation in place, it's easy to break down the learning into modules and lessons, and teach each step on the journey towards the overall goal.

You don't have to stop there; you could use part of your model to create further courses within your area of expertise. Using the *Automated Business System* model, we could create an entire course delving into the details of strategy, for example, or create a mini course around pricing or automation. Each new course allows us to provide added value to our existing audience while saving the trouble and expense of attracting new clients.

There are endless combinations based on the elements of your model, but the rules are the same for each course: describe your client transformation from having a problem, to problem solved; and map out your teaching to lead them to their goal.

> ## What next? Action steps

1. Use your expert model to describe the modules of your course, arranging them in the order necessary to maximise the chances of success.

2. For each model, design a lesson plan for every element your clients need to learn. Describe the learning outcomes for each lesson, using a verb to describe what your students should be able to do once the lesson is complete.

3. Decide on the format you would like to use to deliver your course. If you use video, will they be screen presentations, direct to camera, or a mixture of both?

4. What activities will you include in your course?

** BONUS **

To download the Course Creation Worksheet and see your course plan in one place, and other FREE Bonuses, visit
www.DontSleepOnItBook.com/Bonus

Chapter Five

Pricing Your Course

Perhaps the reason price is all your customers care about is because you haven't given them anything else to care about.
—**Seth Godin**

C hoosing a price for your course can be one of your most difficult decisions as a business owner. Getting it right requires thought and strategy.

The price of your course will affect the type of marketing you can do to promote your course, to the type of students you attract and—perhaps most importantly—the amount of revenue you can generate.

But if you get it wrong, this isn't necessarily a disaster. You can keep changing it until you hit exactly the spot between what your market is willing to pay and what makes sense for your goals.

Charging too low

Charging too low erodes the perceived value of your course and will limit your revenue potential—as well as your marketing abilities. In general terms, selling your course for a low price is a bad idea.

Whatever you charge, you will still need to market your course and persuade your prospective buyer to part with their cash. When you aren't making much money from your course, it's hard to motivate yourself to market it. It takes just as much effort to sell a low priced course as it does to sell a high priced one. Why invest a lot of time and energy into something that's giving you only a small return?

And it isn't true that people will buy something *just because it's cheap.* Whatever price they pay, they will still want to know what they're getting for their money and still want something of value to them.

Most people inherently know that you get what you pay for. Therefore, if you sell your course at too low a price, you degrade its perceived value. It's better to position your course as the premium option in your market.

Just because it's online doesn't mean the training offered is less valuable than in-person training. Many people value the convenience of online training and are actually prepared to pay *more* for it. A higher course price attracts more qualified and more committed students.

Competing on price is a race to the bottom. There will always be someone out there who can charge less. Let them. Clients who are chasing the cheapest option aren't the kind of clients you want, anyway. It's better to focus your marketing on people who respect the value of what you have to offer. People value things in proportion to the price they've paid for them. If your cost investment is low, there's a fair chance they won't complete the course, and an even higher chance they won't implement what they've learned.

The problem is working out how low is too low. This depends on a variety of factors, including your course topic, your market, your authority and credibility and your marketing costs.

If you charge too low for your course, this can show you have a lack of confidence in it. Rather than charge a low price, it's better to look closely at your course content and work out what changes you need to make so you can offer value to your target market.

Exceptions

There are a few scenarios where charging a low price might be a good idea. For example:

- **During a pre-launch testing period.** Pre-selling your course before its official launch can help you get started. This is a good tactic if your course isn't ready yet (so long as your students get access to your course as soon as it is released). During the pre-launch period, you can get feedback that will enable you to tweak your course.

- **When you have a deadline before a price increase.** When you set a deadline after which the price of your course will go up, it acts as an incentive to buy now. Deadlines create a sense of urgency. However, you need to be careful not to go too low.

The video courses offered by YourPregnancyDoctor mentioned above are of higher production quality than most would typically offer. They aim to reach the masses and so have opted for a lower price point so there is work widely accessible to millions of prospective and new mothers. They sell each video course (60+ minutes of content on each course) for just £24, offering a bundle discount if you purchase all four.

Setting the right price

It can be difficult to work out what to charge. Some people choose to start off at a low price point, gradually increasing the price until they find what works best for their market.

This is a valid approach, but it takes a long time to get it right. It's easier to take a bit of extra time considering all the factors involved so you can get the price right (or at least, nearly right) the first time. As Randy Gage says in his book *Mad Genius,* 'Not everything you try will work, but that's not the point. The point is that you're in the game, doing things, moving forward. You'll learn as much from your failures as from your successes. Celebrate it all.'

- **Don't price your course based on its length.** The value of your content is much more important than how much there is of it. However, your students are going to expect a certain amount of content based on the price they pay— they won't be happy if you charge them £200 for a fifteen minute video.

- **Check the competition.** Knowing what people are willing to pay for similar content is really helpful. However, don't fall into the trap of thinking you need to choose a price point somewhere in the middle of what's available. Checking out the competition shows you market demand and what people are willing *have* paid, not necessarily what they *will* pay. (It can be helpful to purchase a competing course to see what's on offer so you can ensure that your course is different, better and offers more value.

- **Quantify the value of the outcome.** Think about how long it would take your client to gather the information you're offering on their own. How much money would they have to spend? What do they gain from your course? The alternative options may be much more expensive and time-consuming, meaning your course could be perceived as a bargain.

- **Consider your credibility.** If you already have a recognised platform and you're your name is familiar to your target audience, they'll be more willing to pay a premium. For example, if you've published a book, spoken at conferences, been featured in the media, received any awards or can offer positive testimonials, you can probably charge a higher price for your course.

- **Clarify your objectives.** What do you want your course to do for you? You might view it mainly as a money making venture, or perhaps it's a resource for customers of a different product or service you offer. Once you know your goal, it's much easier to achieve it.

- **Calculate the cost.** You need to factor in the costs of producing and selling your course if you're going to make a profit—and that means factoring in *everything* involved. It can help to create a spreadsheet for all of the expenses you accrued when developing your course, plus the costs that will come later such as hosting.

Premium pricing

There are plenty of people who will pay a premium for high-quality information that's convenient for them to access. They're prepared to pay for access to an expert and will implement what they learn. These are the people you are creating your course for. Premium pricing attracts serious clients—and these serious clients want to know you're offering value. There are numerous ways by which you can increase the perceived value of your course.

- **Teach something very specific:** Usually, the more specific your course, the more you can charge for it. Your course will stand out among the competition and clients are likely to be more invested in the outcome.

- **Include downloadable resources:** The ability to download lessons gives students more control over their learning experience. Or you might want to add support material such as worksheets, templates, checklists and resource guides. All these increase the value of your course.

- **Offer a payment plan**: People like to defer payments, especially at higher price points. Although they might not be able to afford paying for a course upfront, staged monthly payments (for example) could attract people to your course who otherwise thought it was too expensive.

- **Offer a completion certificate**: Completion certificates validate your clients study experience and increase student engagement.

- **Create different price tiers:** People love to have different options to choose from. Lots of research suggests that having three options and focusing on the middle one is very effective at increasing sales. Some people choose to have a free trial version, although a low-cost version can have the same effect of giving people the chance to evaluate options and choose what's best for them. Instead of choosing between you and a competitor, they focus on choosing between you at one price and you at another price. You could offer bonuses for your second and third tiers such as a members' online forum or extra content.

It can often take more work to sell at a higher price point, but the return on investment will be much better.

Arvind Devalia sells his programme, as of writing this, for £6,000. That's why he needs to invite potential clients to a call instead of selling directly. That way, he can see if they are a good fit to work together. He typically requests payment upfront too.

Another of my clients, Zoe Kennedy, sells her LinkedIn Leads Done for You service at £7,000 for three months (targetedleadz.co.uk). Zoe, the founder of Targeted Leadz and the creator of The Profit Leadz System, spent five years working in the construction industry, establishing brands using just the LinkedIn platform. She launched her first LinkedIn training product in a joint venture with serial entrepreneur and internet marketing wiz Matt Bacak, where they successfully hit the top spot receiving 'Deal of the Day' on the buying and selling platform Warrior Plus—where she made 500 sales in the first week!

When it comes to offering different price tiers, a good example is Tony Be, the author of *Your Greatest Wealth: 9 Steps To Optimising Your Health & Happiness*. His programme which is designed to help you 'Recover And Maintain Your Health The NATURAL Way!' has three plans for purchase: Standard, Upgrade and Your Greatest Wealth Package. In addition to the learning modules with video lessons and worksheets, the higher grade plans include intolerance testing, mineral testing, tablets and capsule packages that are mailed to the customer's home for an all-round support programme.

Finding your price sweet spot

The first thing to remember is that you aren't alone. Every course creator had no clue how to price when they started—but the successful ones soon found out.

How?

First, check out the cost of similar courses, but this isn't enough. When looking at how someone else prices their courses, you have to remember that all courses aren't created equal. You need data.

The important people are the ones who are likely to buy your course—it might sound obvious, but some people ask everyone *except* their potential clients. A focus group or questionnaire would help you find out this information.

- Survey your audience to see if they'd pay for your course
- Ask them if they'd pay £XX for it

If at least a third of your respondents say yes to that price, you can go higher. Remember, only a very small percentage of your audience will buy your course, so if a third of the people you survey say they'd buy at the price you suggest, chances are you can go higher.

Although you might find out you're the only person offering a course in your area of expertise, that doesn't necessarily mean people will pay more for it. While it's often true that you can charge more for a course no-one else is offering, it might be that there's so little interest in that subject that it will only sell at a lower price point.

But none of the following are reasons for pitching your price low:

- **You don't feel you're expert enough.** There's always going to be someone who knows more than you. The question is whether you know enough compared to people who'll buy your course.
- **They could learn it on their own:** Maybe they could. But why would they want to when you've gathered all the information for them?
- **Somebody else is already teaching your course topic for less**: But people who sign up for your course want your perspective.

It can't be said too often—it's less about the price tag and more about the perceived value of your course. As long as you can convince people that your course offers what they want, meets their goals and is convenient for their lifestyle, they'll be more than willing to pay a premium price for that.

What next? Action steps

- Research online courses on the same (or similar) subject to yours. Make a note of the price of these and what you get for your money. Do they offer good value?
- Run a survey to find out if potential customers would be happy to pay the price you have in mind.

Chapter Six

The Sales Process

The easiest way to make money is—create something of such value that everybody wants, and go out and give it; the money comes automatically.

—Jordan Belfort

With a clear picture of what motivates your clients, an expert model in place and your course ready to be sold, the next stage is to attract clients to your product and encourage them to buy. Obviously, without paying clients you don't have a business, yet it's surprising how many entrepreneurs are either uncomfortable with pushing their product, or unsure how to proceed.

In this chapter, you'll learn how to construct an automated sales funnel that draws people towards your product through a process of giving value, building relationships and increasing trust. Starting by capturing your clients' attention, the process follows a predetermined sequence of steps that ends the moment a purchase is made. Implemented correctly, a sales funnel:

- **Is product specific**—it allows you to focus on a particular problem and ideal outcome without boring clients who don't have that problem right now.
- **Is generous**, beginning by sharing valuable information regarding your client's problem and continuing to give until they trust and believe you have the solution they need.
- **Includes action steps**, asking your client to make small commitments that set them on the path towards their goal. By doing so, you help your client get excited about something that will improve their lives and feel it's actually possible to achieve their goal.
- **Removes the need for pushy sales** by increasing engagement with the problem, building interest in finding a solution and helping your client trust you'll provide the expert help they're looking for. By the point your client reaches your sales page, they will be ready to make the purchase decision alone.·

In this chapter, I'll outline the framework—or skeleton—of a successful sales funnel. I'll also show you which elements of the process can be automated to free your time for the parts of your business where you're most needed.

The skeleton of an expert business sales funnel

A sales funnel is a carefully planned sequence of emails, videos, webinars, downloads and interactions that lead your prospect to become a client. The exact choice, combination and sequence of media depends on the type of client you're serving. A sales funnel is complete with a seamless purchase process and automated follow-up sequence, giving clients access to the product they have paid for.

The word 'funnel' suggests a linear, leads-in/clients-out process where you start as a stranger and end up with a sale. But a highly effective sales journey (the process of generating, capturing, nurturing and converting leads) is cyclical, drawing your clients to buy further products as you deepen your relationship, build trust and present new offers.

At *Automated Business System,* our clients base their sales funnel on a proven model that allows them to consistently engage, nurture and serve prospects and clients.

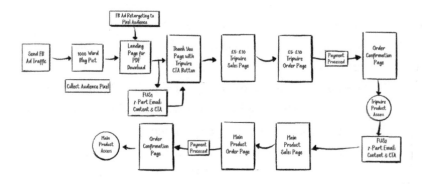

This funnel structure is ideal for turning visitors into prospects and prospects into clients. It is made up of the following key stages:

Lead generation

The first step in the sales funnel is lead generation. This is where you use marketing to raise awareness of your product among your ideal client group, and help them get to know you and get value from you, so they're interested in taking steps to find out more. It is important to create a consistent message across the channels that reflect your ideal clients' values and speaks directly to them.

Once a person has indicated their interest, they become a 'lead'. You may have sold products previously or already have an audience from a previous venture, in which case you can generate leads from an existing list.

Lead capture

Lead capture refers to the invitation for people to enter your sales funnel by way of collecting their contact information in exchange for a free product that helps them move towards their goal.

The best way to do this with new prospects is to first send them to a content magnet—a 1,000 word article, or a video or audio recording typically found on your blog or website that's attractive to your potential client. It provides information to help them immediately alleviate any struggle or challenge they might be facing. The content magnet is available free on your website—it's easy to find and doesn't require the visitor to opt-in for it. The barrier to entry is absolutely zero and it makes the perfect piece to warm the reader.

For example, Zoe Kennedy of Targeted Leadz focuses on finding large businesses that want to use LinkedIn to generate leads. She drives advertising traffic to an article on her blog entitled '8 Reasons Your Business Needs LinkedIn'.[5] Zoe asks, 'While there are countless social media sites out there, LinkedIn has always been promoted as the professional platform—but do you use it to its best advantage?' and then goes on to describe why businesses should use LinkedIn.

Similarly, Tony Be drives his Facebook ads traffic to his blog article, '5 Powerful Strategies for Coping with Chronic Illness'[6] In this, he offers a number of strategies for dealing with chronic illness, ending with a link to his health programme Your Greatest Wealth.

---

5   targetedleadz.co.uk/8-reasons-business-needs-linkedin
6   yourgreatestwealth.co.uk/5-powerful-strategies-coping-chronic-illness

Prospects typically need reinforcement of your brand before they buy from you. That's why sending them to a content magnet is also a great way to get cheaper cost-per-clicks from your paid advertising campaigns. You can build up a large audience to whom you can later retarget secondary ads which send people directly to your lead magnet, and that way obtain higher conversions. (This is covered in more detail in Chapter 9).

The next step is to direct prospects (through retargeting) to a landing page with one single purpose—to capture your client's information and give them something they need in exchange. Even if it is a single insight that opens their eyes to new possibilities, make your information useful, preferably life-changing in a small way. Trust is an extremely valuable commodity that must be earned. Don't be tempted to give them half an answer in your lead magnet then expect them to pay to find out more.

Jay Abraham says in his book *Getting Everything You Can Out of All You've Got*, 'If you want to become the most interesting person in the world, you need to become the most interes*ted* person in the world,' observing that people are most drawn to those who are most interested in them. The same goes for trust. If you can give people value *before* they become paying clients, trusting in their journey and their integrity, you will earn their trust in return.

Lead capture is not sales, but it still involves your client taking a leap of faith to step into your sales funnel. Whether you use a short opt-in box or a long-form sales page, it's worth investing effort in high-converting copy, without confusing or distracting prospects by giving them any other option than to sign up or say no.

Your landing page

Your landing page is any web page that a visitor can 'land' on. It's usually a standalone web page distinct from your main website, designed for one objective. And it steers visitors in exactly the direction you want them to go.

Landing pages need to be much simpler than other web pages. They have specific goals and shouldn't include distracting or irrelevant information. Therefore, any text on it should be clear, concise and persuasive. Similarly, you usually only need one, or possibly two, images. You want to avoid visual clutter—in fact, anything that detracts from the call to action.

Larger font sizes work well as long as you don't go overboard and put everything in a headline-size font. Centred, single-column landing pages work best. The look of your landing page should reflect your brand. That means using the same colours and fonts you use elsewhere.

Although most people who visit your landing page are already interested in what you have to say (they've shown that by clicking through to it), that doesn't mean they'll stay interested if you don't get to the point. Every single word on your landing page should support your call to action. If it doesn't, it shouldn't be there.

A powerful headline is essential. It captures and retains attention and can increase conversions by up to 400%. Clarity rules, so you should refer to only one goal and show an easy way of achieving it. That means spelling out what you want and making it easy for your visitor to find and click the button that will take them to the next stage. Although some visitors will be happy to scroll down to read more information, others will be ready to buy as soon as they arrive on your landing page— make it easy for them. And to cater for those who like to check out every detail before committing themselves, make sure calls to action appear at regular intervals on your page. Again, you want to make it easy for them.

Similarly, ask for the minimum amount of information you need. There's no need to request a phone number if you're only going to contact them by email. Keep everything as simple and concise as possible. The more information you ask for, the more likely it is that your visitor will move on. People are protective about their information so having a privacy policy set out clearly promotes trust and increases conversions.

It's also a good idea to get rid of unnecessary navigation, for example, a link to your 'about' page. This is to limit the options available to visitors, helping to guide them toward your conversion goal. All you need is your call to action, and possibly a link to more information. Anything else clutters up the page and increase the chance of visitors leaving.

It can help to include social proof—statistics, graphs, testimonials from previous clients—anything that highlights the value of what you're offering.

All of this is much easier if you have a clear goal. In fact, a clear goal is essential. Without it, there's no way to create an effective page. You also need specific expectations on which to gauge your landing page's success. These expectations could be based on a variety of factors including experience or anecdotal evidence. Ideally, you'll have a specific number to compare your results with (for example, the total number of conversions or the number of people who make it past your landing page).

Lead magnets

Useful (and therefore valuable) lead magnets include:

- **Video:** there isn't anything to match video for creating an instant emotional attachment and encouraging action from your client. However, be warned—video should be designed for short attention spans. Try to stick to a single purpose and move your client towards an action step at the end.

  Tim Harper of LiveToSki.co offers a video on three mistakes most skiers make on the slopes and how to avoid them. The five minute video names and illustrates these mistakes before describing how to correct them to avoid injury or tiring too fast. Having delivered this valuable information, Tim invites clients to sign up to his paid course to get more of the same or similar.

- **Email content:** A short sequence of emails is ideal for increasing awareness of a problem, while encouraging engagement in the form of daily calls to action that move clients towards a particular goal.

Joey Romeu created his Power 2 Perform Fitness training programme to help people get fitter, leaner and stronger. His client's journey begins with a seven-day 'Re-energiser' email course to encourage small lifestyle and mindset changes to help them start burning more fat, increasing their energy, and improving their performance. Each day introduces a new topic and keeps clients focused on their goal by setting an achievable action step.

Don't be tempted to bombard people with emails. Although the frequency of how often someone will be willing to receive emails from you will vary according to what the emails are about, two or three emails in a week is usually ample. Plus, your emails don't have to be epic, either. When in doubt, shorter is almost always sweeter.

- **Checklist:** This is my personal favourite. A checklist is typically one to three pages, a pleasure to look at and easy to digest. It's appealing to sign up for, too.

  Ronald De Keersmaeker, founder of the *Impact Academy*, helps professionals become better at speaking, negotiating and selling. For each of these three segments, he has an individual checklist he can promote as a lead magnet. For example, one of his lead magnet checklists is a two page PDF entitled, 'The 10 Step Checklist For Persuading Any Audience.'

Lead nurturing

After giving you their details, the third stage, and a key part that runs throughout the entire sales funnel is lead nurturing. Ryan Deiss sums this up in his book *Invisible Selling Machine* when he says, 'A potential customer has given you permission to contact them. This is a big deal! Now what? The first step is to teach your new prospect about you, your company and your brand. You need to indoctrinate them. Who are you? What do you stand for? Why are you different? What should they expect from you? How often? What should they do next?'

A nurturing campaign builds momentum towards your clients' desired outcome and increases their confidence in your ability to deliver. Usually, this is an automated sequence of emails combined with various calls to action, such as watching a video or webinar, downloading further content or booking a free coaching call.

When setting up a sales funnel, it can be hard to know how much to give away, in case the client signs up, takes what they need and disappears. This happened to me when I set up a paid membership service in my music company, giving clients access to all my content in one go. After the first (heavily discounted) month, the vast majority had downloaded everything and unsubscribed! This was one of my biggest business mistake to date. I won't be using that business model again! Nevertheless, I still advocate giving exceptional value even in your free content.

There will always be people who take what you give them for free and not buy. They might believe they can do it on their own, or they take longer to trust you, or you're simply not the right match. It's possible they can't spare the money. However, if you come from a place of absolute service and give them information of real and lasting value, they may come to you later or recommend your product to somebody else. Keep trusting, and you'll earn their trust in return.

My nurturing campaigns are built on the principle of *know, like and trust*: I give clients the opportunity to get to know me and decide if they like me, while offering quality content that builds their trust. Understanding your client is essential. The closer you get to your client's needs, wants and desires, the closer you get to their heart, and the more chance you'll have of winning trust and signing up new clients.

In my regular newsletter and my autoresponder sequences, I:

- **Avoid jargon, sales talk and BS.** I regularly make clients aware of what I can offer them, but direct them to a landing page. My email content is for providing valuable content, not hard sales
- **Give solid, useful information,** not intangible fluff
- **Share as many case studies as possible,** demonstrating the success of my offerings while giving prospects an insight into what they can achieve
- **Give personal examples.** My struggles and successes tell my clients what's possible for them
- **Tell them what to do next.** I include a call to action at the end of every contact, whether it's an actionable task for their own business, or signing up to further content

Leading up to a sale, clients need clarity about what you offer, and complete confidence that you are the person who can help them. Every single point of contact should work towards this goal.

At minimum, a simple funnel like the one shown above, will have a tripwire product and a main product, and will need the following minimum number of nurturing campaign sequences to support this.

- The first email sequence is sent to prospects who have requested the lead magnet and are now receiving your emails, inspiring them to take action and buy your tripwire product.

- The second email sequence is sent to customers of your tripwire, guiding them to take the next step and purchase your main product.
- The third email sequence is sent to customers of your main product, encouraging and supporting them on their journey, and perhaps making supplementary offers.

Of course, it doesn't matter how great your emails are if no-one opens them in the first place. Therefore, you need to ensure that your subject line encourages them to do just that. Almost half of all email recipients decide whether to open an email based on the subject matter alone.

To make your email stand out, your subject line should:

- **Communicate urgency:** This can help compel readers to take action—if done creatively and strategically. You have to follow-through though, so limit these subject lines to when the occasion calls for immediate action. If you're creating urgency, it's important to keep your email short and to the point. Otherwise, you'll fail to keep your recipient's attention.
- **Tell them what's inside:** If your recipient has downloaded an offer and you're delivering it, it's best to use a subject line that says something like 'Your ebook Is here!' rather than 'thank you' or 'order received'.
- **Pique curiosity:** If your subject line interests the recipient, they'll want to open the email to get more information. If you make an allusion to a story your message tells that can only be read if the email is opened, your audience is likely to want to learn more. Or you could ask a question that will be answered in your email. However, try to avoid being too obscure.

- **Make an offer:** People love new things and experiences, especially when they're free or at a discount.
- **Be personalised:** There are plenty of ways to learn about a subscriber's preferences, and they'll be far more interested in your email if it reflects those. At the least, it's a good idea to address people by name. Emails that include the first name of the recipient in their subject line have been proven to lead to higher click-through rates than emails that don't. However, be careful not to go overboard with personalisation or you'll look as if you're stalking the reader. Even if you don't use their name, you can still address the reader as 'you' so it sounds as if you're addressing them directly.
- **Be relevant and timely:** Email subject lines that incorporate current trends or timely headlines help you establish your brand as an authority.
- **Have name recognition:** You can pique your reader's interest by including the names of recognisable individuals.
- **Avoid spam wording:** Some words are automatically caught by spam filters. Try to avoid words commonly used in spam emails such as 'clearance', 'income', and 'claim'.

Whatever you put in your subject line, don't make false promises. Your recipients will soon unsubscribe if they feel conned.

Using action-oriented verbs tends to be a lot more enticing and inspires people to take a look. However, SHOUTING AT PEOPLE IN ALL CAPS or overusing exclamation marks is a good way of making sure your email is ignored!!!!!!!!!!!

Florence West is an executive coach who works with employees at corporations in the US. She writes an email newsletter every week to share content and promote her programmes. In her experience of writing newsletters for the last three years she knows for a fact that shorter subject lines, specifically less than 28 characters, get the highest open rates. Her top five subject lines are:

'X options to get started' 39% open rate

'Where is the love?' 34% open rate

'Fight for your dreams' 27% open rate

'FREEDOM' 42% open rate

'For your eyes only...' 39% open rate

Often, it's a simple matter of rephrasing. For example, if you're sending an order confirmation, 'Your order is being processed' is better than 'Order #9435835893458 for your ebook is currently being processed.'

If you want to stand out among the hundreds of emails your audience receive each day, you need to remember that first impressions matter. You could spend hours crafting the perfect email, but that's useless if no-one opens it in the first place.

Tripwires

People need to have trust in you and your product before they'll spend a significant amount of money. And you need to find a way of building a relationship to create that trust. One way I recommend of doing this is with a tripwire.

A tripwire offer is a way to entice customers to your brand. It's something that costs little to produce and requires little commitment. It takes advantage of people making impulse purchases. Once the customer has bought the tripwire product, they have entered the sales funnel. You can then lead them further along the funnel, and finally sell them your higher priced main item. As the tripwire gets people into the funnel, it increases the likelihood of that individual buying your higher-priced products. People are taken through a series of micro-commitments, each bigger than the one before, and they become repeat customers.

Once people have bought even a cheap item from you, they are more likely to purchase something else. People tend to be suspicious when faced with free offers and wonder what the catch is. A low-cost offer helps remove that suspicion.

Tripwires also help offsets traffic costs. Most people run paid ads when generating leads. These leads will turn into profit in the long term, but don't make any money upfront. With a tripwire offer, you can recoup some of that advertising money.

There are numerous options for a tripwire, but they all have a few things in common:

- It's small
- It's easy to purchase/download
- It's related to your core product
- It still provides great value to your clients

An easy way to work out what you can offer is to break down your main service or product into components and sell one of those components separately.

For example, Norva Abiona created a mini course called *The Successful Warrior Queen*[7] which still provides great value to her clients yet allows them to explore and engage with her as a client, rather than remain a prospect. It includes a forty-five minute video course and a worksheet.

Other possibilities include:

- A guide in the form of an ebook
- Access to a short video or course

---

7   riseof.thewarriorqueen.com/warrior-queen-thank-you

- A 'need to know' checklist on a pdf
- A small gadget related to your product
- Webinar
- A plugin or app
- A trial period

The key is to focus on something very specific.

A crucial part of this strategy is to price your tripwire so low that it's hard for your prospective customer to say 'no'. For example, many companies give the product away for free and only require their customers to pay for shipping.

Once you've made the sale, you should link your offer to your main product. For example, saying ' Now you've read the guide to XXX, find out more by purchasing XXX.'

Tom Mitchener runs Head2Web.com, a simple, affordable service to help you manage and run your website and search engine campaigns. As part of the SEO services they offer, they run a three monthly packages but they also have a tripwire which is an SEO audit service[8]—it offers a comprehensive audit of your website and advice on how to increase your rankings. This is offered in the form of a report and a consult provided for one low flat fee of £29 +VAT. The interesting thing is that the phone consult provides an opportunity to speak to a buyer and upsell their monthly retainer services.

The idea with a tripwire isn't to make a profit (many tripwires are sold at a loss to bring in customers), it's simply an introduction to what you have to offer. You could offer a deal on your product while the customer is purchasing the tripwire or email out an offer on your core product separately.

---

8   tom.head2web.com/seo-audit

Lead conversion

As you nurture your leads, they should receive regular invitations to visit a sales page that invites them to buy Lead conversion is the process by which your lead will become a customer.

A high-converting sales page is one where your visitors will follow through to make a purchase. Inevitably, there has been a large amount of research into what helps a client convert. (Note that a landing page asking a client to sign up for certain lead magnets benefits from applying exactly the same principles as this—whether you want them to hand over their personal details or their credit card details, the process is the same):

- **A compelling headline.** If the title doesn't catch your clients' attention, your work is wasted. Make sure it reminds the client what they're signing up for, keeping their eye on the goal!

  The landing page for Dr Julie Coffey's monthly subscription service introduces 'Accountability, Advice and Support To Help You Stay Healthy, Slim, And Full Of Energy For Just 32 Pence A Day.'

- **Offer only one thing.** Rule number one—keep your prospects' eye on the ball by having a single focus for your entire page. Avoid navigation and don't confuse matters by upselling or cross-selling here. Your client is here to buy. Make it as easy for them as you can.

  In order to sell his Ultimate Life Transformation System programme, Arvind Devalia runs a free webinar where he talks about the mental shifts people need to make in order to achieve important and meaningful goals. He then walks them through the programme he offers and he has one single call to action: *book a call with me to see if this is right for you.* He doesn't push them to buy from the webinar, nor does he talk about the price. He simply wants them, if they are interested, to book a call and discuss whether they would work well together. Interestingly, once someone gets on a 'free strategy call' with him, he has a high close rate.

- **Include a call to action.** Whatever you want your client to do, ask them to do it! This may sound obvious, but I have seen too many business owners make the payment link small or obscured. Include a big, bold button that's impossible to miss.

  Norva Abiona does just this on her sales page for her *Rise of the Warrior Queen* course.[9] The page describes the course interspersed with buttons you can click to register. There's one simple offer and no room for confusion.

- **Include evidence.** People are reassured by social proof, in the form of testimonials, case studies or statistics backing up your claims. A powerful landing or sales page will include as much factual information as possible to dispel any remaining doubts your client may have.

  Healthletix filmed their clients talking about the personal transformations in fitness/health they have had a result of working with the programme. These short videos appear on the website and sales pages and provide evidence to prospective buyers.

  Zoe Kennedy compiled a number of case studies about her previous clients and their experience of using her LinkedIn knowledge. These studies show who the client is, their industry and how many leads she acquired for them in a ninety day time frame. And they show she gets the results she claims.

---

9   riseof.thewarriorqueen.com/warrior-queen-course

The Psychology of Persuasion

In his book, *Influence: The Psychology Of Persuasion*, Robert Cialdini explains six emotional triggers that influence human decision making. I teach my clients how to put these six triggers to work in their sales pages to dramatically increase their conversion rate:

1. **Reciprocation:** If you do somebody a favour, they will feel obliged to return the favour at some point. By the time your client reaches your sales page, they should have enjoyed your lead magnet as well as further valuable content bringing them closer to their goal.

2. **Commitment:** As humans, we prefer to believe our choices are good, therefore we'll continue to commit after an initial decision has been made. Each time your client interacts with you, the urge to commit will increase.

3. **Social proof:** People tend to act on the example of others, so evidence of previous clients using and succeeding using your system simplifies the decision-making process for new clients.

4. **Liking:** If we like a person, we're more likely to trust them. Clients won't make it to your landing page if they don't like you. You don't need any clever sales language at this stage, carry on as you are.

5. **Authority:** As a society, we tend to look for leaders and trust them to take us where we need to go. Having reassured clients of your expertise, it's OK to advise why taking your course is the right move. Associations with other recognised authorities, such as industry leaders or trusted platforms in your field, also increase trust.

6. **Scarcity:** Humans are more decisive in the face of scarcity. People will buy quickly faced with limited availability or running out

of time. More subtly, you can imply that the longer they delay, the longer they'll have to wait to see results.

If you're anything like me, your alarm bells are ringing like crazy right now. These tactics are used to pressurise, manipulate and coerce desperate punters into buying anything from Viagra to SEO services in spammy sales pages and unsolicited mails. If you're feeling uncomfortable, great. These triggers should be used sparingly and with integrity.

However, if you've created a course that will get your client the results they're looking for, you're doing them a disservice if you don't do what is necessary to help them make the decision to buy. Understanding the psychology of sales can help your client get over the objections that hold them back from success.

The examples below detail the sales process for a few of my clients.

Example 1

Emma Teggarty and James Crew of *Elev8 Business*[10] (which helps fitness professionals set up a successful personal trainer business) use a sales funnel to promote their book and online programme. Clients who arrive on their landing page are invited to sign up to an exclusive series of three videos (their lead magnet) which deliver business insights and action steps to help a struggling personal trainer build a business that delivers their dream life. Each video introduces a new concept and offers an exercise or a download to engage prospects with the idea of creating business success.

The landing page and the first two videos are followed by a follow up sequence (FUS) of three emails to prompt the client to watch the next video. The final follow-up sequence is seven emails—one every five days for thirty-five days. This sequence continues to nurture the prospects, leading them towards the sales page.

10 elev8business.com

The sales page also includes a video, this time ten to fifteen minutes long, but it has no other purpose than to explain the benefits of the product and inspire clients to click 'buy'. All additional action, including entering their personal and payment details, happen on the order page which follows.

Once payment is made, clients are redirected to a confirmation page with immediate access to their product in the members area of the site and information describing what happens next. They are also sent email confirmation of their purchase and invited to set up a member account.

Example 2

Life coach Arvind Devalia set up a sales funnel to promote his Ultimate Life Transformation System, which he currently sells for £6,000. The first step, the lead magnet, is a webinar, In this he talks about his ULTS Expert Model and how to balance the differently moving parts to achieve a fulfilling and ambitious life.

This sales funnel relies less on email, as a forty-five minute webinar is used to dig deep into the value of the investment the client will make. Once drawn to the landing page, clients are encouraged to sign up for a free webinar at their preferred date and time. The first follow-up sequence reminds prospects of their commitment with up to three emails to ensure they turn up to the webinar.

After the webinar, a follow-up-sequence of seven emails (once every five days for thirty-five days) thanks clients for their attendance and leads them to the sales page. If the client signs up, the emails stop. After payment, clients are redirected to a confirmation page outlining what happens next. They also receive an email confirmation and, if appropriate, are invited to the members' area of the site.

Example 3

This example is for someone who sells a high priced product or service. At a higher price level, clients need more information to be sure the investment will deliver the results they need. This funnel has to provide evidence and an opportunity to have a telephone conversation to explore their questions and concerns.

We use this sales funnel for *Automated Business System,* beginning the process with a case study video which lets a client's success story speak for us. On the landing page, I introduce the case study and invite clients to find out more. Once they've opted in, they are led to the full-length video where our clients explain why they wanted to set up an automated business, the process we took them through and the results they achieved.

The case study video invites prospects to schedule a free coaching call with one of our business startup coaches, and the first follow-up sequence reminds them of their appointment and provides further case studies to build trust.

During the coaching call, we provide as much value as we can, but this call is also designed for both parties to decide if they're a good fit. If the client is happy, we can give them the information they need, answer any additional questions and provide details of how to proceed.

The final follow-up sequence (again, seven emails over thirty-five days) kicks in if the call didn't close the sale. The emails thank them for the phone session, acknowledge they didn't buy and provide further content and case studies to strengthen the possibility of a future sale. At any point, the client can go to the order page and sign up to *ABS.*

We have helped over 135 businesses launch using *Automated Business System,* so we have a strong track record to support this sales funnel. It's still possible to launch a high-ticket product as a new business, replacing the case study with a webinar explaining the benefits of working with you, like Arvind did in the example above.

Example 4

This example is for a recurring membership product that allows experts to offer valuable and exclusive content and access to the experts on a group basis. For an expert, this is a rewarding business model. People who continue to use this service after the free trial get the most value from working with you and are the most dedicated to achieving results.

Dr Julie Coffey provides the *Uber Health Club* for people who want further accountability, advice and support in addition to her paid online course. She provides weekly Q&A calls, recipes and motivating success stories to keep her clients on course to their healthy lifestyle, as well as other exclusive content from time to time.

The sales funnel for a continuity programme starts with a valuable lead magnet such as a downloadable ebook or report. Clients are directed to a thank you page, followed by an email sequence to build a relationship with the subscriber, helping them to know, like and trust Dr Coffey's information and her personal style.

Prospective clients are regularly invited to a sales page, which includes a fifteen minute video exploring the benefits of membership, with an invitation to a no-obligation free trial. On the subsequent order page, clients can choose from a monthly or an annual payment and enter their personal details.

As before, at whichever point the client makes a purchase, clients are directed to a confirmation page, given further information and all subsequent stages of the sales funnel are stopped.

As you can see, sales funnels don't happen by chance! A high-converting, automated sales funnel requires careful strategy and step-by-step content creation as well as the technical know-how to ensure your client is continually nurtured and doesn't hit any dead ends.

However, this a proven formula that, once established, can attract, sign up, reassure and commit new clients non-stop, at all times of the day and night.

What next? Action steps
---

1. Consider which sales funnel model is the best match for your course, based on your pricing and business model (such as subscription or single purchase)
2. Identify what you need to create for each of the four stages of the sales funnel skeleton. Include your lead magnet, plus every email and video script.

** BONUS **

To download 3 Lead Magnet examples, and a
60-minute Email Marketing Masterclass video course to
complement this chapter, and other FREE Bonuses, visit
www.DontSleepOnItBook.com/Bonus

PART THREE

MARKETING YOUR COURSE

Part Three focuses on marketing your completed course, exploring how to lead your clients into your sales funnel already knowing something about you and trusting in your ability to give them what they need. You'll learn, with examples, about the different marketing options available and how to use them to boost sales and reinforce your expert brand.

These chapters contain a lot of content. I recommend reading them through before returning to each chapter and completing the action steps I provide. This information is worthless if you don't put it to good use!

Chapter Seven

The Marketing Relationship

One of the biggest challenges an entrepreneur or innovator has is understanding how to make his ideas resonate. We tend to have no shortage of ideas, but we struggle to tell the story of how they are going to be useful in the world and why they will matter to people. Marketing is the way we communicate how our ideas translate to value for people in a marketplace.

—Bernadette Jiwa

M arketing is about the transfer of passion and emotion about your product and service from you to potential clients. It is the process of building a long-term relationship with your clients by making sure they know about you, then helping them warm to you and find it within themselves to trust you enough to buy. Without marketing, your clients will likely have no idea you or your product exist—even if they did, they would have little reason to care. Like Gabriel Weinberg says in his book *Traction: A Startup Guide to*

97

Getting Customers, 'Almost every failed startup has a product. What failed startups don't have are enough customers. This is what we call the 50% rule: spend 50% of your time on product and 50% on traction.'

Everything in this book comes back to one core concept—holding your clients in the highest regard. This starts with being interested in what troubles them, what's important to them and what they want out of life. It involves digging deep into your own expertise because it matters to you that they get results. And it involves letting them know (and helping them believe) you have a solution to their problem—you *want* them to overcome it and you believe in their ability to do so.

This is why marketing is so important it gets a whole part to itself. All the effort and energy you invest into creating a course means nothing if you don't let the right people know it's out there and is intended for them. It's a wasted venture if you don't help them get over their resistance to take this first important step towards achieving their goal.

Stages of a marketing relationship

In Chapter 6, I split the sales funnel into four distinct stages: lead generation, lead capture, lead nurturing and lead conversion. At each of these stages, the client is in a different stage in their relationship with your brand and on their journey towards purchasing your product:

- **Awareness:** At the lead generation stage, your client's problem is brought to their attention and you make them aware your product exists to solve it
- **Interest:** Lead capture happens when the client expresses an interest in solving their problem
- **Decision:** Lead nurturing is the process of leading the client towards a purchase decision by helping them get to know you, learn to like you and trust you have the solution they need

- **Action:** At the lead conversion stage, the client takes decisive action and enters their credit card details to gain access to your course

Marketing plays a role throughout the sales funnel. It helps the client become aware of your product, and draws their attention to a problem the product solves. It is used to generate enough interest so they click on a link or sign up for your lead magnet. And it continues throughout the lead nurturing process to help your client make the decision to buy.

It's important to note that each sales funnel has a single purpose—to lead a customer towards one product. However, just because a funnel is focused on one product, it doesn't mean you have to continually search outside your network for new clients. Your marketing efforts before, during and after a sales funnel help build a bond of trust between you and your clients, so the same person can be drawn to multiple sales funnels, each for a separate product that solves a different problem.

This is where marketing differs from sales. Great marketers are in it for the long haul, building relationships and nurturing trust. Ben Chestnut, co-founder of email marketing platform MailChimp, describes the traditional sales funnel as a grinder, taking new leads and churning them through the one-size-fits all sales machine until some emerge as customers and the rest disappear.[11] In contrast, Ben's 'upside-down sales funnel' begins with loving your clients and accepting that some will try your product and some won't. This love leads to an engaged audience who will happily share your love with their friends.

---

11 tinyletter.com/ben/letters/why-i-hate-funnels

While your marketing should aim to attract your ideal client as defined in your customer avatar, a long-term marketing vision doesn't dismiss anyone who doesn't immediately buy, or use newsletter sign-ups to launch straight into sales. If someone trusts you enough to give away their personal details, it's essential to repay that trust, not spam them with every offer you have.

Ideally, your marketing should build a solid relationship with your clients—you can draw attention to your offers, but if they don't buy straight away, trust in the process and keep providing value until they do.

Golden rules of marketing

There are certain marketing behaviours that are more effective than others. To build a loyal following and avoid investing money, effort and time on the wrong audience, you'll need to follow four golden rules:

- Interact (turn an 'audience' into a 'tribe')
- Build trust
- Be consistent
- Analyse and learn

Interact

Back in the days when TV and radio advertising were the only way to reach a mass audience, marketing effectively meant broadcasting a message then waiting for people to come to you. Today, people expect highly personalised content and an almost immediate response from any business they interact with. Responding promptly can boost your reputation for good service, but responding *personally* turns an anonymous audience into an engaged community with a shared bond.

Acknowledging, listening and giving a genuine answer to comments on your blog, or queries and complaints via email or on social media allows you to show your clients they matter to you. To encourage interaction, ask questions, run surveys or invite them to tell you what content they need. Seth Godin says in *Tribes: We Need You to Lead Us*, 'Marketing is the act of telling stories about the things we make—stories that sell and stories that spread.'

My YouTube channel shares four- to seven-minute long videos, each of which covers one key topic in the areas of productivity, marketing or sales funnels. If I receive a great question from a client, I often respond with a new video so everyone can benefit from the answer. Not only is the client over the moon with the personal response, but encouraging new questions also gives me an endless source of content ideas!

Build trust

This is the fundamental principle driving my entire marketing strategy. Trust builds engagement, both among your ideal clients and a wider community who, while they may not benefit personally from your products, could refer you to your ideal client at any time. If your clients can't trust you, your sales funnel will fail.

Use your marketing efforts to help your clients trust that you:

- **Care.** If your clients get one sniff of being treated as a walking pay cheque not a real human with genuine problems and concerns, they'll unsubscribe and may even give up on their goal. In contrast, when you act from a genuine vision of changing their circumstances for the better, you will give your clients the courage to take the next step.
- **Want what's best for them.** This could mean being willing to direct them elsewhere if you think another expert can serve their needs better than you.
- **Can deliver the goods.** Your clients come to you expecting you to help them become better versions of themselves.

Therefore, every area of your marketing from social to content, ads to partnerships all need to focus on helping your clients become better versions of themselves before they do business with you. Creating immediate feelings of momentum towards transformation is the surest way to build trust.

- **Will do what you say.** Keep your promises. It's better not to commit yourself if you don't think you'll follow through. Of course, we're all human so if you forget or overcommit, a simple, heartfelt and honest apology will go a long way.

Clients may give a rational reason for purchasing your product, but most people buy with their hearts and justify the decision in their minds afterwards. A heartfelt decision becomes much easier if you have established trust.

Be consistent

Consistency is an important step towards building trust. If you only deliver sporadic content, regularly change your message, or don't focus on a central theme, your audience won't be able to trust you when you promise results.

Your expert model gives you a huge scope for different courses and a wide range of content which can be confusing for you, never mind your client! The thing that ties it together is your vision for your business and what drives you to do what you do.

Your core business story is made up of four parts:

- **Purpose:** Why you're here in the first place, the problem you're here to solve
- **Vision:** Your long-term vision for a future, and your clients' success

- **Values:** The things that matter to you, that guide the way you approach your work
- **Plan:** How you intend to bring your vision into reality

The more you can weave this central story of your business into your marketing messages, the easier it is for a disparate collection of products and content to appear cohesive and purposeful to your clients. It helps reassure them you are here for the long-term, are purpose-driven and have their best interests at heart.

Three marketing strategies

So where should you focus your marketing efforts? This is an important question because each of us has a limit to the amount of money, effort and time we can spend on marketing. If you are clever, you can re-use or share much of your content on different platforms, but it still pays to focus and not spread yourself too thinly.

I advise my clients to begin with one channel each from three main marketing types: online advertising, content marketing and social media. Each serves a valuable purpose in building relationships, building trust, driving people to your sales funnel or generating new leads, meaning the combination is a strong foundation for growing your business over time.

Online advertising	Online advertising is a quick way to guide more traffic to your site, but can become expensive very quickly. You need to ensure it performs in the way you want it to by using the right strategy.
Social media	The key to making social media work for you is remembering that it's social first and involves engaging with people.

Content marketing	Content marketing focuses on creating and distributing valuable, relevant, and consistent content to attract and retain a clearly defined audience—and turn many of them into clients.

Online advertising

Display or banner ads often come to mind when we think about online advertising because they stand out so much. Although they can be effective, they are commonly used as a 'retargeting' mechanism, reaching out to people who have already visited your website and enticing them to return.

There two most common solutions available for running successful and profitable online advertising campaigns are:

- **Google AdWords** which offer display and text ads in association with highly targeted keywords.
- **Facebook Advertising** has grown enormously during the last few years. These ads combine text and display elements and are targeted based on user preferences, demographics, and location.

You'll probably want to try both options and analyse the results before you make a final decision about how to invest your money. One big advantage of online advertising is that you get the opportunity to track everything. There are plenty of tools available to help with this, for example, Google Analytics (which is free) and Kissmetrics (a free trial is available). You will not only be able to see the amount of traffic you've received from the ad but also how many clicks converted into a genuine lead. Traffic alone isn't enough. With some ads, you might have a lower click count but a higher percentage of those clicks converting to sales.

Chances are, you won't get it right first time, but it's easiest if you make only one small change at a time. That way you can see if it brings any results. With online advertising, the longer you run your ads, the better it does. This means you need to be ready for the long haul. The costs soon mount up, so it's important to set a budget and stick to it. In Chapter Nine, we will look at Facebook advertising, my preferred choice, in more detail.

Content marketing

The key to content marketing is that the content has *value* for its audience—ideally, it's something people seek out and want to consume. The goal is to provide as much value from your content marketing to as much of your target audience as possible. Content marketing can take a variety of forms:

- Webpages: Not all webpages are content marketing, but those that offer information, tools and access to resources often are.
- Blogs: Your blog can offer up to date content as well as provide a venue for you to connect with potential customers. It also helps set you up as an authority in your industry.
- Podcasts: A podcast gives you a different sort of visibility. It allows you to share audio regularly, potentially reaching a huge audience, especially those commuting to and from work listening through their earphones. With the rise of audio devices like Alexa, this is a great opportunity to release content that is easily accessible.
- Video: Whether it's a short film captured on your mobile phone or you commission a film from a video production company, the premise is the same. A video allows you to *show* what you want to sell rather than just *tell* people about it.
- Infographics: These include statistics, charts, graphs, and other information. Those that grab people's interest can be passed around social media and posted on websites for years.

- Books: Many marketers sell or give away books as marketing tools. Even if you don't sell many, you will still have the kudos of being able to say you're the 'author of...' which helps you to establish credibility and brand awareness in your industry.

Content marketing allows you to increase people's awareness of what you offer and what you stand for. You can offer them a solution they need while pointing them in the direction of yet more solutions that will help them achieve their goal. Once someone has realised they need a solution for their problem, they will begin to search for it. And when they do that, they could come across your content.

YourPregnancyDoctor.com is a good example of a content-rich website. This is a vast learning resource for women looking to get pregnant or already pregnant. The site contains over 450 articles that anyone can search through in categories and subcategories to get the help they need, free of charge. (This website is only open to the UK market.)

Social media

The key to making social media work for you is remembering that it's *social* first. Engaging with people, being responsive to questions and being regularly involved are imperative whatever platform you use. Of course, there's no need to restrict yourself to one platform. They work in different ways and appeal to different audiences. However, there is a large crossover between social media platforms, so this needs to be borne in mind when planning content. For example, a video on YouTube may appear on people's Facebook pages or Instagram account, and if it gains enough interest, people will tweet about it.

Sam Oke runs the majority of his business on LinkedIn. As he offers the LinkedIn profile rewriting service, he typically mines and finds his clients and gets awareness for his work on LinkedIn, specifically reaching out to people that have lesser quality profiles.

———————————

Your choice of platform will depend on your personal preferences, the type and purpose of your content and where your ideal customers can be found. In the following chapters, we'll look at each of the above in more detail.

Chapter Eight

Social Media Platforms

Social media is about the people! Not about your business. Provide for the people and the people will provide you.
—**Matt Goulart**

Social media is the perfect way to reach an enthusiastic, highly engaged audience who are looking for information in your area of expertise. Social media channels are also a perfect platform for interacting with your clients, building trust with a wider audience who will see you via their friends' activities.

For example, I have a Twitter profile where I generally share valuable curated content from other experts, interspersed with links to my own blog or YouTube channel. This is usually content that offers another angle on sales funnels or business building, or something that has inspired me that I'd like to share. I allow this platform to direct my clients to valuable information without having to generate more content myself. This also helps clients trust I have their best interests at heart.

However, my YouTube channel is perfect for hosting compelling, targeted video content that clients are likely to engage with and share. YouTube has powerful search capabilities which allow me to connect my content with keywords or questions my clients might ask, such as 'How often should I email my list with sales offers?' It also hosts my content, which I can embed in my blog and Facebook posts.

Moz.com analysed engagement on their own blog and found that people are 50% more likely to share content on Facebook and Twitter if it contains video, so I consider this a valuable use of my marketing budget and time.

To get started with social media, choose one platform that suits the kind of content you intend to produce, and where your ideal clients are most likely to be found. Include your chosen platform in your overall marketing strategy, regularly linking to your blog or any lead magnet offers you wish to promote.

Instagram

In September 2017, Instagram announced that it had 800 million monthly users, of whom 500 million used the site on a daily basis.

Creating a business profile allows you to add additional information about your business on your profile and promote your Instagram posts. It also offers free analytics for your Instagram account. This will provide you with (for example) follower growth, details on when your followers are most active, and information on your top-performing posts.

One of the best practices for growing an Instagram account is to post consistently. This doesn't necessarily mean posting frequently. Once or twice a day works well, as the more often you post on Instagram, the more likes and followers you gain. However, posting more often might not always work—especially if you do it on a temporary basis. Your audience might not be used to seeing several posts per day from you and you might not have the time to create that amount of much content and maintain quality. Too many posts can actually be annoying and cause people to stop following you. Posting consistently is more important, preferably sticking to a regular posting schedule.

There isn't a single best time to post on Instagram. However, posting consistently at the same time of day works well. You also need to think of the needs of your audience. A lot of people check their social media at lunchtime so this can be a good time to start.

Remember to include a caption to what you post. This enables you to mention another Instagram account and add hashtags. Accounts that you mention will receive a notification and your post will appear when someone searches for the hashtags you used. Hashtags are the norm on Instagram, and increase engagement. You should include up to 30 hashtags per post. Tagging people can also be helpful. And if you have connected other social media profiles to your Instagram account, you can share your posts on those profiles.

It's usually best to use a short caption as Instagram only shows the first three lines of a caption and hides the rest behind a 'more' button. Ideally, it should be 125 characters or fewer. Keep the crucial details at the start and place hashtags etc. at the end.

Once you've set up your account, you will be prompted to 'find people to follow.' You can connect your Facebook account, your contacts, or follow profiles suggested by Instagram. However, it's often better to search for stories and posts that fit with your brand. By searching a keyword relevant to your business, you will find relevant profiles. As you begin to follow more profiles, Instagram will make further suggestions. You don't necessarily need to connect with people who have huge numbers of followers. Often, it's more relevant to connect with those who have smaller followings but a high level of engagement and who are active influencers. Check out their account.

Similarly, you need to make it easy for people to follow you. Make sure you mention your Instagram profile on your other social media profiles and that you add a link to it on your website or blog, It's also a good idea to include your Instagram username on your name cards. When people follow you on Instagram, you'll receive a notification. Check out their profiles and follow them, too.

Obviously, not all your followers will become clients. However, if you get more followers, you'll get more leads. Like all social media, Instagram is about engaging. When your followers comment or ask a question, it's important to respond as quickly as possible. People are more likely to use a product or service when they've received a response on social media. Like Guy Kawasaki says in *The Art of Social Media: Power Tips for Power Users*, 'Sharing good stuff is 90 percent of the battle of getting more followers. Almost everything else is merely optimization.'

One way of engaging followers is to feature customer photos on your account. If, for example, you were selling a course on dressmaking, you could encourage followers to post photos of their creations they'd made after studying your course. They will share these photos on their personal accounts and potentially gain you even more followers. User-generated content increases the likelihood of engagement and therefore of drawing people to your website.

Instagram stories

Although Instagram is primarily used to post photos and videos, you can also post stories. Instagram stories are photos and videos that disappear after twenty-four hours. Verified accounts can add a link to their Instagram stories to drive people to their preferred website. Unlike normal Instagram posts, Instagram stories don't appear on your profile gallery or your followers' feed but are hidden behind your profile photo on a separate feed. Stories can be used to:

- Tell a story
- Explain how to do something

- Promote a blog post
- Share a list
- Announce a promotion (the most common use for businesses)
- Offer discounts
- Share an statistic
- Share a quote
- Make an announcement
- Host a competition

Instagram Stories tend to generate more views for brands than Snapchat Stories and are a good way of receiving a direct message reply.

Although videos have become more popular on Instagram, photos still make up the greatest number of posts. Whether videos or images are best for you will depend on your followers, so you may need to experiment. However, videos on Instagram tend to be very short—on average about thirty seconds.

My own posts are a combination of short video clips from talks or done as recordings for Instagram, and quote images from my talks. These get interaction and help me grow my following, and people typically click on my bio link to go to my website. I post two or three times per day on Instagram.com/kavitharia.

YouTube

YouTube is by far the largest video sharing site with over a billion users. Those users account for over four billion video views a day. YouTube videos are integrated into Google search results, and if you watch a video on Facebook, there's a fair chance it's a YouTube video. Every kind of audience accesses YouTube, which means any business can benefit from marketing on it. However, few businesses invest in YouTube marketing.

People watch videos because they want to learn something or they want to be entertained. (Ideally, your video will address both needs.)

Because it hosts user-generated videos, YouTube is often referred to as a social network. Indeed, the success of a YouTube video comes from people sharing it with friends, usually within the first few days of launch.

Tutorials, guides overviews and reviews are ideally suited to YouTube. People love watching online videos, and sharing informative content tells their friends they are knowledgeable. These shares are what will ultimately drive your video's traffic until it creates organic search traffic. It's impossible to predict whether a video will become viral, but there are ways to increase the chances that a video will get shared.

The content of your video needn't necessarily be directly related to what you are selling so long as it addresses your target market. Once you have gained their attention, you can direct them towards your course.

If you want to make sure people can find your video on YouTube, you need to think carefully about using the right keywords. People like plenty of details when it comes to video content, and the longer and more detailed your video description, the better you'll rank for relevant searches. Also, provide as much information as you can when uploading your video—it all helps to improve visibility.

Interacting with your audience will help build a community around your YouTube content. That means interacting with them on other social media platforms and making sure people can connect with you. Always ask for feedback and respond to comments both within YouTube and elsewhere.

Not all your feedback will be positive. You can safely ignore troll comments that are just posted to get a reaction from you. However, honest comments can be an opportunity to learn and improve your future videos.

Sometimes your videos may need a little push. To increase your potential audience, you could use YouTube's own ad service 'TrueView in-stream'. This is the skippable pre-roll ads you see at the start of videos. TrueView also offers 'in-display' ads which appear as a thumbnail and text on YouTube watch pages, or 'in-search' where your video appears in a special section of the video search results pages on YouTube and Google.

When you upload your video can be important. If you plan (for example) a weekly series, it's best to upload your video on the same day each week. That way, people know when to log in to see the next one.

YouTube recommends organising videos into three categories:

- **Hygiene:** Simple and clear videos based on high volume searches in your category, for example, a brief tutorial.
- **Hub:** Regular, scheduled videos that give viewers a reason to subscribe and keep coming back.
- **Hero:** One-off events designed to increase your audience's growth.

It can take time to build a good profile on YouTube—possibly a few months before you start getting large numbers of organic views. It might be demoralising, but don't give up if a few videos fall flat.

YouTube looks at a number of factors when ranking a video.

- How much of the video most viewers are watching. If they drop off after the first few seconds, that's a bad sign. But if more than half watch the whole video, that's a different matter entirely. (You can check this in your account's statistics.)
- The number of overall views,
- Views to subscribers: If a video is really good, a lot of people who view it will click the 'subscribe' button.
- Views to favourites or social shares.
- Comments: YouTube doesn't put too much weight on the comment count as comments can be negative.

You don't necessarily need thousands and thousands of views to rank well, but you do need to find a way to get your first few hundred views. Once you start getting more subscribers, you won't have to focus on promotion as much.

Although your video may be hosted on YouTube, that doesn't mean it should be the only place it can be found. The same video can be linked to your blog, website or Facebook page.

Views are obviously important, but it's easy to forget what the point of creating a YouTube channel is. It's to increase your sales. Through YouTube you can get the attention of potential customers and then the next step has to be to get them onto your website and onto an email list. Encouraging viewers to subscribe means they will get notified of your latest videos, and a number will watch all your videos as you release them.

But to get people to your website, you'll need a link. Although you can—and should—add a link to your videos, the best place is your description.

I created 85 little videos and generated 41,116 targeted views from YouTube. When it came to making decisions about creating and developing my own marketing plan, online video quickly became the no-brainer I invested heavily in. I knew that video encourages exceptional results:

- Video content will deliver a far higher engagement rate than written content
- Video content encourages more people to take immediate action
- Video content has a universal appeal that written content cannot match
- On top of that, video marketing content is far more likely to be shared on social media than any other type.

As example of this, the hugely respected search marketing company Moz.com analysed engagement on their own blog. They found that:

- Text only blog entry was shared via twitter around 700 times
- An entry that also contained a video clip was shared via twitter around 1100 times
- Text only blog entries were liked on Facebook and average of 480 times
- Blog entries that contained a video clip will liked on Facebook and average of 639 times
- When all three elements, text, images and video were contained within a blog post, the average share rate on Facebook and Twitter was over 1200 times.

My own 85 short video blogs have been viewed a total of 41,116 times. This has brought me more than 700 new email subscribers. Those subscribers have helped to grow my business, especially in allowing me to help people through my Automated Business System, essentially driving the success of my online business.

When it comes to information, people generally have short attention spans unless they are captivated by what they are consuming. The internet has allowed people to develop a highly refined visual, auditory and emotional information filter. In terms of video content, although you have the instant-win of faster engagement than written content, that can quickly tail off. To avoid losing watchers before that all-important call to action is made, you need to make sure that your video content is:

- Short in duration—around 2 to 5 minutes
- Highly targeted
- Packed full of information
- Straight to the point

- Compelling
- Results-focused

The second rule is that as well as being short, your videos must make a single and compelling point. The information you deliver must be precisely around what the viewer expects and it must be fresh. The third rule about creating high converting marketing video content is to make sure you do it regularly.

When somebody views one video they may like it enough to subscribe to view the next one. But you have not build trust at that point. It will take time to build that relationship, which means making sure they know when you are going to deliver content that builds it. So produce video content that is as regular as clockwork for maximum benefit.

People want answers to questions and solutions to problems. To produce video content that people can't get enough of, you need to know what burning questions or problems they have. This means understanding what people are searching for online, by researching your niche using basic keyword research techniques.

It's about more than that though. You may have seen one of the endless 'OK Google' TV ads recently. This new use of voice searching, mixed with mobile browsing means search terms are now more conversational than they used to be.

My top tip is not to just do classic keyword research, but also to brainstorm around the types of actual questions people might ask. Put yourself in their position and generate lists of verbal questions you might ask. These are great for forming the basis of titles and content within informal, conversational style video content.

Another great way to find out what people are looking for content on is to.... ask them. I like to do surveys, using tools such as Survey Monkey to get answers from interested people. You can promote the surveys using social media, or an existing mailing list, or pay per click advertising. However you do it, the answers you get will be gold dust—giving you powerful information to produce video content that matches the exact needs of ravenous buyers who are looking for reassurance.

Recording great video content is easy, unless you choose to make it difficult. Video becomes difficult if you over complicate and overstretch yourself. Video content is easy if you keep things simple.

- **Keep it visually simple:** Use a blank background and you or a presenter in front of the camera. You can then use one or two static cameras and cut the angles in using basic video editing software.

- **Keep your lighting simple:** Lighting is something that is overlooked often. Getting it wrong can destroy a great video. Consider filming outside. How do you cope with the light changes of a six hour shoot? Simple means shooting indoors.

- **Keep your presentation style simple:** Simple makes powerful more easy to achieve and allows you to connect with more of your audience. If you are concerned about presenting your own videos then there are ways around this. Get some coaching, get a professional presenter, use visuals with narration. Ultimately it will be your decision on how important it is that you personally connect with your potential customers.

- Publish your video content on two powerful platforms: It's essential that you make your video content the centrepiece of your own website. You don't have to have massive bandwidth issues by hosting the video yourself; you can upload a video on YouTube and then embed it into your articles. This will give you two main channels for people to touch base with your content on. Each piece you publish on your website should put the video front and centre, and support it with other information.

Calls to action, additional details, images, will all add to the power of your post for social media sharing.

However, the chances are that unless you are very established then you will only see a trickle of views and actions taken. This is why a long-term marketing strategy for every piece of video content you make is essential. Don't just think in terms of sharing it on social media such as Facebook and Twitter and telling your mailing list about it.

For every piece of content you create:

- Develop at least a three month marketing plan
- Aim to hit different aspects of this plan in a staged, progressive manner
- Revisit each stage to refine and re-promote
- Be ready to instantly exploit opportunities

When it comes to exploiting opportunities, I'm talking about adopting content when you get success. Let's say that you produce a two minute video clip on a topic that goes viral in your niche and starts to produce a good stream of regular views on conversions. That's the opportunity you need to spot and immediately exploit.

Take the content of that video and make another video based on the topic. Or reuse footage from your initial session to cut a new version. Bundle it up with a free lead generation report and create a new landing page. Push people from the existing video to the new landing page.

Never view a piece of video marketing content as the end of its journey; always be vigilant for opportunities. Acting on feedback can be the difference between success and failure

As well as acting on success that you spot yourself, you can turn around a failed video by taking on board any feedback you receive. As an example of this, after producing around thirty of my own video blogs, I analysed the feedback I was getting and found I was regularly being told people wanted to also read the content. So we began to create written transcripts and offer them below the video. On top of that, we tested something else:

If people wanted to download the transcript then they could do it through an opt-in form, allowing me to harvest more subscribers.

A vital part of your follow-up marketing is about listening to what people tell you and acting on it rapidly. If they want more information, get another video done and push it out to those people. The more you engage, the more you build a relationship, the more you will enjoy loyalty and higher conversion rates.

Right from the day I started, I chose YouTube as my preferred hosting solution for videos. It was free and I could make my video content part of the entire Google and YouTube search engine.

After I'd created about a dozen videos, I started to really get into learning about YouTube and playing around with many of their features. For example, I created my own playlists and grouped my videos together which meant that my visitors could choose ANY category and get theme-specific content served up. I also began to study the YouTube Analytics. I could see which of my videos had the most views—telling me what people searched for the most, or what they may mostly be interested in. I could even tell exactly where these people came from (the traffic source). What was interesting to note was that the YouTube suggested video provided the highest traffic—more than even embedding the video on my site and driving my own traffic. Even the playlists provided traffic.

An intelligently pitched piece of video will engage with all types of people who are interested in what you have to offer. Video can stir emotions and provoke in a way that the written word can't. The ability it has to generate rapid understanding, more instantaneous exploration and quicker decision-making make it ideal as an online sales conversion tool.

Twitter

Twitter might not seem an obvious choice when it comes to content marketing. However, with over 330 million users in September 2017, it's much too big a platform to ignore.

It's easy to set up a Twitter profile, What isn't so easy is turning your account into a useful tool. It takes more than simply sending out tweets to announce a new product or upcoming event. Again, you have to engage with your audience. Like Randy Gage says in his book *Mad Genius,* 'Rather than simply trying to get more followers, you need more *engaged* followers. Add quote. Don't pander to the masses. Speak to the people you really want to reach and be honest. Challenge them to do more and become better. And know that if you're not attracting some haters—you're probably not doing something significant.'

One way of achieving this is through Twitter chats. People who participate in chats are those who enjoy engaging on Twitter—and these are the types of people who will respond to your tweets and retweet your content.

To start, look for Twitter chats related to your niche. If you can't find any, set up your own. Twitter is about contributing. Also, remember to reply to other chatters—don't forget to @mention them so they're notified. And follow up by retweeting, favouriting and replying to their tweets and sharing their content. This is just the start of your relationship.

At least a third of your tweets should be in response to other people. It's all about being conversational, which means higher engagement. And being responsive could result in new clients. A lot of businesses just make announcements and don't open the door to further communication. If you tweet a link, add a comment of your own to get the conversation going. If you tweet an image, say something about it.

If you just tweet links to your content, most people won't see it. You need to space out your tweets to improve your visibility.

Although video isn't the first thing that comes to mind with Twitter, it offers a couple of options for using video. Its own video feature allows you to record videos up to 140 seconds long and upload them directly to your Twitter stream. Alternatively, you could use Periscope, which is a live streaming app owned by Twitter. Once the stream is over, the recording is still available for people to watch. And don't forget—you can also share slides and photos.

Because Twitter moves so fast, it's important to figure out when your own followers are online—that's when you tweet. To analyse when your tweets get the most engagement, you could use Audiense, Hootsuite or Tweriod.

When Twitter is used well, it can a lot of traffic to your website. However, it isn't enough to simply tweet the title of a blog post with a link back to your website. To maximise the effect of your posts on Twitter:

- **Keep it short:** Tweets that are 100 characters or less tend to get higher conversions. If you post a link, you don't need to add more than a brief introduction.
- **Quote your post:** Posting a teaser from your blog can pique curiosity.
- **Use @mentions:** If your blog mentions anyone, make sure to mention them in your promotions. There's a good chance they'll share your tweet.
- **Ask for a share:** Tweets that ask for retweets often get them.

If you're still not getting the engagement you want, you can pay for promoted tweets. However, allowing your followers to grow organically by joining in what's happening will be far more successful.

What next? Action steps

1. Set up an Instagram account and create your strategy by deciding on what content types to post, your frequency and what times you'll post.
2. Set up a YouTube channel and write a list of videos you could begin to create and shoot.
3. Set up a Twitter account and start following people in your industry or niche.

Chapter Nine

Facebook Ads Funnel

Nobody counts the number of ads you run; they just remember the impression you make.

—Bill Bernbach

Facebook ads are a powerful, must-use tool for all online businesses.

Although all social media is effective whesn it comes to getting more impressions, clicks and conversions, Facebook stands out—it's cheaper, has billions of daily active users, and allows you to target users by location, age, gender, interests, behaviour and more. Your campaigns are easy to track, you get an immediate influx of traffic and always have complete control over your budget.

Tim Harper used a Facebook advertising strategy to build the audience on his Facebook page. Being a complete Facebook novice, Tim excelled himself, gaining his first 3,600 engaged followers in seven months. He advises new entrepreneurs to get their page working well before putting money behind their posts—he ensured his page looked attractive and professional, his business details such as a description and website address were easy to find, and he already had engaging content for his new audience to find.

Many businesses have lost their Facebook accounts due to their underhand marketing tactics and I want to help you ensure you do it the right way

People don't log onto Facebook ready to buy something. It's first and foremost a social space, and it has its own rules. Those who market aggressively with the intention to take from the community rather than serve it will at the best be ignored. Or someone will leave a nasty comment forever damaging their reputation.

Facebook is a great marketing tool but it's not about selling. In other words, you can use Facebook to help re-establish or enforce a position in the market. That will help your sales but it doesn't directly lead to a sale. Facebook is more subtle than that. For example, instead of diving in and shouting about how wonderful you are at what you do, you could share a video or post a photo of you actually doing it. You can share your message in a more laid-back way.

The key to being thought of as a trusted authority is to supply great content. Once you've established yourself as an authority, you can then start reaching into the market with ads to lead to action.

The strategy

Having worked with hundreds of clients and run dozens of Facebook advertising campaigns, this two-step approach is what I have found to work the best. This strategy works to reduce your cost per lead as much as possible whilst giving you the highest conversions.

The first step is to set up an advertising campaign that promotes your 'content magnet' (as discussed in Chapter 7). This is typically a video or article directly related to your target audience and that offers to solve a problem right away. By adding what's known as a Facebook pixel to your website code, you will be able to notify Facebook which of their users has visited your website and you can begin to collect a pool of users who have already engaged with your video or article. This pool is known as a Facebook Audience.

This first step is typically a broad advertising campaign reaching as wide as possible yet remaining focused on your target market's interests, location and demographics.

The second step is to run a retargeting advertising campaign simultaneously. You will have come across retargeting endless times. For example, if you've been to a website online but you didn't buy, and then you hop onto social media and begin seeing ads for that same website, you'll probably have wondered how they are following you around…

Once you have connected with a user on Facebook, you can market to them again and again. People who've liked your content once will catch your updates. Obviously, you can't guarantee they'll see your message, but a reasonable proportion will, especially those who turn on notifications. The key is that when retargeting you are appealing to an audience you've already engaged.

In this second step, you will run a retargeting campaign, aimed only at this new Facebook audience you've collected in the first step, but now focused on driving them to your landing page to subscribe to download or receive your lead magnet.

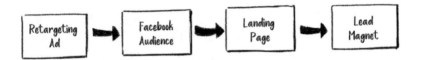

How to choose your advertising audience

To make your Facebook advertising effective, you need to select the right audience. And you can be really specific. This is where Facebook advertising is truly powerful.

After you've chosen the type of ad you want, you'll reach the audience settings tab. This allows you to create a custom audience and target by:

- **Location:** This allows you to include or exclude people who will see your ad based on their location. You can choose to target people who live in the area or those who've recently visited it. You can cover a wide area or be really precise, for example by using a postcode.
- **Age:** You can choose a minimum and maximum age and your ads will only be shown to people who are in that range.
- **Gender:** The default is 'all' but you can choose to target men or women only.
- **Interest and behaviour:** This is the most detailed section of options. Facebook splits this section into three categories comprising 'demographics' which includes educational level, job titles, relationship status and income level; 'interests' which includes fitness, shopping, sports and business; and behaviour which covers purchase behaviour and recent homeowners, amongst other categories. To narrow this down, you can add a segment that all potential audience members need to meet.

- **How someone's connected (or not connected) to your page:** This can be useful if you're trying to track down an audience that might not be familiar with you or follow-up with an audience you've already connected with. For example, it allows you to choose between people who like your page and friends of people who like your page. Or you can choose to exclude people who already like your page.

Or you can choose to create a custom audience of people who have a previous relationship with you as customers or contacts and serve your ads directly to them.

To do this, click the 'create new custom audience' link at the top of the audience settings page. A popup will offer you three different ways to create your audience:

- **Customer list:** You can upload or copy/paste email addresses, phone numbers, or Facebook user IDs. Facebook also integrates with MailChimp so you can use existing MailChimp lists to create a custom audience.
- **Website traffic:** Facebook can create an audience based on the conversion pixel you've installed on your site. You can choose a timeframe for the traffic or segment by (for example) anyone who visits your site or people who have seen particular pages.
- **App activity:** With this, you select one of your connected Facebook apps and segment based on activity within the app.

Once you've created an audience, you can save it for future use.

Four Tips for Your Facebook Ad Creative
- **Start with a goal:** Once you know what you want to achieve, you can style and format your ads to achieve your goal. For

example, you could tell a story about the people behind your products or show people using your product. Facebook ads often run in people's newsfeed next to posts from family and friends, so you should try to create ads that feel like a familiar part of someone's social fabric, and not just focus on your product.

- **Less (text) is more:** Too much text is distracting and might be ignored. Uncluttered images have a greater impact.
- **Stay focused:** Don't try to include too much information. Crop tightly around the important part of the image. If you really need to include a lot of information, you could use the carousel format to show off multiple images in a single ad. If you're running multiple ads in a campaign, make sure all your images have a consistent theme.
- **Use high resolution images:** You don't necessarily need a professional photo, but make sure you pay attention to the size and quality of the media files you're using. There are size recommendations in the Facebook Ads Guide.
- **Experiment:** Play around with different images and formats before you commit to a particular ad, and always—always—preview how your ad will look before you run it. You could also create mock ups and get feedback as well as spend some time looking at what other advertisers produce.

When it comes to advertising on Facebook, it takes twenty-four to thirty-six hours to optimise any given ad. (It's tempting to stare at your computer and watch every lead, but that won't make it work any faster.) Once Facebook has given you the lead cost, you need to first decide if you're happy with it or if you want to reach more people. If you choose to scale up, you'll reach a point where as soon as you raise your daily budget, it will throw off your Facebook algorithm and it will need to restabilise.

It's important to be alert to negative feedback. If an ad starts to get high negative feedback, you should turn it off as fast as you can. Otherwise, you risk Facebook thinking that you don't understand your audience and you're breaking rules within the community—you risk your Facebook account.

What next? Action steps

1. Add the Facebook pixel to your website and create your Facebook audience.
2. Create your first broad ad campaign to promote your 'content magnet'.
3. Create your retargeting campaign to promote your lead magnet.

** BONUS **

To download a 60-minute Facebook Ads Masterclass training video to walk you through setting up your own advertising campaigns as discussed in this chapter, and other FREE Bonuses, visit www.DontSleepOnItBook.com/Bonus

Chapter Ten

Content Marketing

Our job is not to create content. Our job is to change the world of the people who consume it.

—Andrea Fryrear

C ontent marketing is not your sales funnel. There may be confusion between your sales funnel email sequences and providing a regular newsletter, but they serve different purposes in your business and require different content.

Your marketing content serves the purpose of building trust and credibility so people who enter your sales funnel already believe in your expert brand. This isn't to say you shouldn't include sales messages within your content, but the emphasis needs to be on providing value for your clients, based on the goals, challenges and pain points you identified in your customer avatars.

Daniel Priestley, author of *24 Assets: Create a digital, scalable, valuable and fun business that will thrive in a fast changing world,* writes,

'Content clarifies your thinking—when you write an article, record a video/ audio or capture an image or a diagram, you are forced to focus on what you want to share with your audience.'

For example, Dr Julie Coffey created her Uber Health Blog when she realised she had valuable information to share about how healthy eating and lifestyle changes helps you lose weight and gain more energy. Initially, she shared the information with family and friends, but word quickly spread and it wasn't long before she had a dedicated following of people who wanted to know more. Now, her blog forms the core of her marketing strategy for her online courses, books and coaching.

According to digital strategist Olivia Allen, companies that blog receive 97% more links to their website and 67% more leads than those that don't.[12] The obvious reason for this is that people visit regularly to read new content, and already trust in your expertise. To take full advantage of this phenomenon, provide consistent and regular updates so your readers keep returning.

To get started, refer to your client avatar to remind yourself who you're writing to. Provide useful information that helps them address their challenges and pain points and move towards their goals. Use your expert model to constrain your content to your areas of expertise.

The need for content marketing

Content marketing isn't just a marketing term. It's an essential component of a marketing strategy. Buyers want creative, relevant and compelling content from the brands that matter important to them.

When you're trying to build an online presence, you need good quality content. But you also need the right content, content that will appeal to your audience.

Good content:

---

12 '6 Essential Workflows for Every B2B Company', madcashcentral.com/author/olivia-allen

- Establishes thought leadership: It's ideal for positioning you and your brand as an industry leader.
- Attracts followers: Content marketing is ripe for social sharing and brand advocacy.
- Advances sales cycles: if you can align your content with buyers' needs, content marketing makes it easier for them to transform from prospect to satisfied customer.

Each type of content has its own pros and cons. You might be thinking about starting a blog. Or perhaps recording a few videos. Before you go any further, you need to consider what will be the best fit for your business and the audience you want to engage.

One practical consideration is how much of a commitment you can make to content creation. Do you have the resources to publish new content on a daily basis or would weekly suit you better? The frequency of posting is less important than the consistency. However, blogs, for example, demand more frequent posting to be successful. If you're not sure you can manage that, it would be better to look at a different format.

- Consistency is needed for: Blogs, newsletters, magazines and podcasts.
- Consistency is less important for: Videos, whitepapers, ebooks, webinars and infographics.
- Consistency isn't critical for: In-person events, guest postings, research reports, books and apps.

Type of content you can create

Not only do you need to consider what format to use, you also need to decide on what topics to cover. Although it's a good idea to research your audience to figure out what kind of content they're most likely to respond to, you won't know what works for you until you start trying.

However, there are certain types of content that tend to attract an audience including content that:

- Tells a story
- Reminds us dreams can come true
- Gives us faith to hope for bigger things
- Reminds us of overlooked things
- Has an unexpected twist
- Reminds us that we matter
- Inspires us into action
- Takes us on a journey
- Makes us laugh
- Makes us cry
- Reveals a secret
- Surprises us
- Encourages us not to give up
- Challenges our assumptions
- Educates and entertains
- Gives us a fresh point of view

This type of content is more likely to be read, more likely to be remembered and more likely to be shared.

You obviously don't need every type in every piece of content you produce. Often, one is enough, although for longer forms of content you might want to use multiple types and move from one to another.

Create a content marketing calendar

Gary Vaynerchuk, author of *#AskGaryVee: One Entrepreneur's Take on Leadership, Social Media, and Self-Awareness,* said 'Put out quality content every day and engage around it.'

Putting out regular content requires planning. Creating a content calendar can appear complicated, but it's actually straightforward. A content calendar is used by marketing teams to plan all content marketing activity. The advantage of using the calendar instead of just a long list of content you plan to publish is that it enables you to visualise how your content is distributed throughout the year. This means you can:

- Plan content around key events
- More easily see where you have gaps
- Make sure you have your content ready in plenty of time to publish

The further ahead you plan, the easier it will be to produce a consistent flow of content that builds your perceived expertise. It also makes it easier to plan around any industry or other events. You can plan content on a weekly, monthly, or quarterly basis, depending on your needs. However, the further forward you plan, the more prepared you need to be to adapt your plans. To build a content calendar:

Identify your topics/audiences: You're probably not publishing content to only a single audience, and each will be interested in different kinds of content. Some of your content will be aimed towards attracting a new audience, while other forms of content could be aimed towards customers you already have. Your calendar will make sure you spread your efforts where they're most needed. You will need to decide how much content you want to distribute among each group. For example, it could be 75% buyers of product A, 15% buyers of product B and 10% existing customers. Once you've worked out how much content you're capable of publishing each month (or quarter or year), you'll be able to work out how much content you should aim to produce for each audience.

Take stock of your content assets: You probably already have a lot of content you can use. For example, you might have slide decks from training sessions that you can re-purpose as blog content. Or you might have a whitepaper that can be rewritten as a series of blog posts. Re-purposing content takes away some of the strain of having to come up with new ideas. Also, remember that a single piece of content asset can also often give rise to several new pieces of content. For example, an infographic can support a blog post or a video.

Schedule, publish, promote, track, and tweak: Regular planning meetings between all involved should be scheduled well in advance of the content being published. These meetings will not only enable you to schedule with realistic time frames, they can also be used to review the reaction to and effect of your content so you can decide if you need to make any changes going forward.

Your list of potential content and your calendar aren't separate. Rather, they should be used together. Events, the time of year and the availability of resources will determine what pieces of content you want to produce and when. Make sure you record all important calendar events which may affect your publishing schedule (for example, Christmas or industry events).

Great content is at the heart of a good online marketing strategy. And the best content is published in the right place, at the right time.

What next? Action steps

1. Identify which two or three types of content you can commit to producing on a regular basis.
2. Identify the frequency at which you'd like to produce and publish them.

3. Create your own content calendar.
4. Get producing!

Afterword

What Will You Do Now?

The best inventions are never finished. Great inventors don't just stand there, rub their hands together, and say 'My work is done here'. They're not Damien Hirst, freezing their creativity in formaldehyde. They keep working furiously to create something even better. It's part love, part necessity. Because if they don't reinvent their ideas time and again, someone else will—rendering their life's work irrelevant, or worse still, extinct!

—Eric Schmidt, Google

At the beginning of this journey, I talked about how addictive it can be to help others achieve success in something that matters to them. This begins with you. You have a responsibility to share your passion and expertise with the world.

We have gone on a journey together to make the decisions that will help you turn who you are and what you know into a leveraged service business model, guiding people to overcome their challenges and solve their problems.

I've given you everything to help you get started in bringing your course alive and raising awareness with your marketing so you can reach more people and make more of a mark on the world. My wish is that you'll step up and give it a try.

Don't Sleep On It! calls you to step up and share what you know. This is not the time for remaining hidden. I believe our lives are judged by the contribution we make to the world, and this book provides a formula for you to package your knowledge and offer it in an accessible way online, whilst providing an opportunity to build a lucrative income. Follow and implement each of the steps in this book and you will have a profitable online business.

It's likely that if you can see this process through to the end, you'll discover more problems to solve and new opportunities to take your clients further forward on their journey. As the world changes, you'll have to change, too—except in this instance you'll be inspired, not forced, to adapt. Once you start, you'll find yourself on a path of creativity and inspiration that will never end.

So what will you do? Will you put this book back on the shelf and get on with your day, or take the first steps towards a rewarding, ever-changing business that gives you more time while you make more of a difference, day-in and day-out?

Each of us has a choice: to either strive to do work we care about or carry on as we are. Doesn't it make sense to throw yourself into your work? To love what you do and care about the people you do it for. If where you invest your time and effort doesn't matter to you, why would you do it? Your days are too precious to spend them simply marking time until every Friday evening, when your life begins.

Mediocrity doesn't always mean underperforming—it's a sliding scale and a state of mind. It means settling in and succumbing to stasis. Mediocrity comes from the Latin words medius, meaning middle, and ocris, meaning rugged mountain. Literally translated, it means to settle halfway to the summit of a difficult mountain.
—Todd Henry

I hope to leave you not only informed, but inspired to do what it takes to create, market and sell an expert course that makes a difference in your clients' lives. It's rewarding to know that you've contributed, you've made a difference, and you've developed a meaningful and profitable business at the same time. As you've seen, it's a lot of work, but I know from experience it's worth it, to stand at the summit and reflect on what you have achieved.

To your success,

Kavit

Automated Business System: Continue the Conversation

The Automated Business System has enabled me to take my idea of an online business from a very messy and amateurish affair to something that is slick and professional. I enjoy what I'm doing so much more as I have confidence in what I'm doing these days.
—Dr Julie Coffey

The *Automated Business System* is a business development programme to help you turn what you know (your expertise) into a strategic, profitable, scalable and automated online business that allows you to reach more people, make more money and make a greater impact.

Our team of experts take you from idea to launch to profitable online business in twelve months. We build your online infrastructure or help you refocus your existing infrastructure if you already own a business. We are with you every step of the way.

The end result is an *Automated Business System* that combines efficient software with the latest, proven sales, conversion and marketing strategies.

How the *Automated Business System* works

The Automated Business System is formed of three key areas: strategy, implementation and marketing implementation. You will be assigned a personal Launch Management Plan that will clearly detail the exact steps we take to help you go from concept to launch and begin marketing activities to help you reach your sales goals.

Stage 1–Strategy

As soon as you begin working with us, your first session will be with our Business Consultant who will get right to work helping you develop the foundations for your online business and the key marketing messages. You'll also complete a branding experience, a deep-dive customer avatar exploration, detailed product plan mapping and sales funnel planning. You'll then have a laser-focused session to identify your strengths and formulate critical success factors, specific marketing strategies and a personalised Marketing Tactical Plan for you to execute. The strategic phase will bring you clarity about your project and lead you nicely into marketing.

Stage 2–Implementation

Led by our Project Manager, the Implementation phase is about bringing your strategic direction and business vision to life. Working with our team of writers, designers, developers and automation experts we'll follow the Launch Plan to build out every part of your business from branding to copywriting, websites to sales funnels, and professional filming to photography.

Throughout the entire Implementation phase, you will be kept informed of the developments and deadlines by our Project Manager. You'll also be invited to give prompt feedback as we progress in the development of your business. Depending on the nature of your business and the sales funnel we feel is best to convert maximum sales, your online business will be launched by 60 days, and no later than 90 days from when you've begun your *Automated Business System* journey.

Stage 3–Marketing

Once you've developed your Marketing Tactical Plan, you'll be introduced to our Marketing Implementation Coach who will coach and guide you to execute the plan through seventeen coaching sessions. In each session, you will review your marketing campaigns, learn new strategies and implement improvements and iterations to help you improve your marketing. We're committed to being by your side for the entire program.

> *As I'm writing this, it is two years since we started this journey and at this point we've passed the million-dollar mark, achieving $1,130,000 in sales. I have to admit I was hesitant to begin, but doing this has been one of my greatest joys. Not only have we made some really good money, but we've also enjoyed the entire experience, working together on our business, travelling and feeling a lot more growth and creativity in our lives.*
>
> **—Dave and Tina**

The *Automated Business System* isn't a free ride. Passion, commitment and a can-do attitude are essential if you want to reap the rewards on offer. You'll have to live and breathe your new business, but we'll be there to support you all the way.

It is certainly possible to go it alone and build a business by yourself. You can access all the information you need; in fact, the most important fundamentals are in this book. However, our clients who have tried this approach (before eventually coming to us) tell us it's tiring and stressful. There's a lot to learn, and a lot more to implement, especially with designing and developing your business model on the web.

We take away the pain and hassle while providing you with the help and support of our team of experts who have a proven record of growing ideas into online success stories.

Next step

On your own, you are vulnerable, but connected to a peer group and advisor team who can give you feedback and accountability, you are unstoppable. If you want to build your own lifestyle freedom online business with the help and support of experienced experts, my team and I are here to help.

We will help you turn your idea into reality by formulating a commercially-viable business model for the web. We design, develop, create and implement all of a client's marketing and sales funnels and launch their business. We also provide marketing mentoring to reach £100,000 in sales in your first year.

The *Automated Business System* is our total end-to-end business transformation system. The first step is to book a call with our Business Coach to discuss your goals, look at how this might work for you and see if we are a fit to work with you. If we're going to work well together, we'll tell you and we'll invite you to join our programme.

Visit www.InsiderInternetSuccess.com/call to book your free session now.

About the Author

From a young age, Kavit learned to play the tabla, a north Indian percussion instrument, and was interested in mixing Eastern music alongside Western music (pop, R&B, hip-hop, jazz, reggae, Latin). Having immersed himself in learning about artist promotion, Kavit began to raise his profile and performed across the UK, playing gigs at venues large and small, with many artists (including Jimmy Page at the Royal Albert Hall) and recorded albums at the Abbey Road studios.

Recognising there was a demand for sharing what he learnt gave rise to Kavit's first company, *Insider Music Business*. Within five years, from 2005 to 2010, Kavit created thirty-five different educational products online, everything from ebooks to video courses and audio training to membership programmes which he promoted to the growing database of 120,000 musicians.

As a result of the success in the music business, Kavit turned to share his marketing automation strategies at business conferences in the UK and ran private workshops for small business owners in New York, Sydney and London.

Since 2013, Kavit has been running *Automated Business System, a flagship service to help experts and brands* strategise, build, launch and market their businesses online businesses.

Sources and Further Reading

Aaker, David A. Aaker. *Aaker on Branding: 20 Principles That Drive Success*. Morgan James Publishing, 2014.

Abraham, Jay Abraham. *Getting Everything You Can Out of All You've Got*. Piatkus, 2001.

Cameron Herold. *Double Double: How To Double Your Revenue In 3 Years Or Less*. Greenleaf Book Group, 2011.

Cialdini, Robert. *Influence: The Psychology Of Persuasion*. Harper Business, 2007.

Deiss, Ryan. *Digital Marketing for Dummies*. John Wiley and Sons, 2007.

Deiss, Ryan. *Invisible Selling Machine*. Digital Marketing Labs, 2015.

Gage, Randy. *Mad Genius*. Tarcherperigee, 2016.

Godin, Seth. *All Marketers Are Liars*. Portfolio, 2005.

Godin, Seth. *Tribes: We Need You to Lead Us*. Piatkus, 2008.

Harnish, Verne. *Scaling Up: How a Few Companies Make It... and Why the Rest Don't*. Gazelles Inc., 2014.

Henry, Todd. *Die Empty.* Portfolio Penguin, 2013.

Jiwa, Bernadette. *Marketing: A Love Story.* The Story of Telling Press, 2014.

Kawasaki, Guy. *The Art of Social Media: Power Tips for Power Users.* Portfolio Penguin, 2014.

Marshall, Perry. *80/20 Sales and Marketing: The Definitive Guide to Working Less and Making More.* Entrepreneur Press, 2013.

Nepo, Mark. *The Book Of Awakening.* Amber Lotus Publishing, 2016.

Reynolds, Garr. *Presentation Zen: Simple Ideas on Presentation Design and Delivery.* New Riders, 2007.

Sinek, Simon. *Start with Why.* CreateSpace, 2016.

Vaynerchuk, Gary. *#AskGaryVee: One Entrepreneur's Take on Leadership, Social Media, and Self-Awareness.* Harper Business, 2016.

Vaynerchuk, Gary. *One Entrepreneur's Take on Leadership, Social Media, and Self-Awareness.* HarperBusiness, 2016.

Walker, Jeff. *Build a Business You Love and Live the Life of Your Dreams.* Simon and Schuster, 2014.

Walker, Jeff. *Launch: An Internet Millionaire's Secret Formula to Sell Almost Anything Online.* Morgan James Publishing, 2014.

Weinberg, Gabriel Weinberg. *Traction: A Startup Guide to Getting Customers.* S-curves Publishing, 2014.

Zander, Benjamin Zander. *The Art of Possibility.* Harvard Business Review Press, 2000.

Printed in the USA
CPSIA information can be obtained
at www.ICGtesting.com
JSHW082339140824
68134JS00020B/1775

9 781683 509851